Keeping Your Kids Grounded When You're Flying By The Seat Of Your Pants

by
Tim Jordan, M.D.
and
Sally Tippet Rains

Palmerston & Reed Publishing Company
St. Louis, Missouri

Keeping Your Kids Grounded When You're Flying By The Seat Of Your Pants

by Tim Jordan, M.D. and Sally Tippett Rains

ISBN 0-911921-42-7

Printed in the United States of America

Published and distributed by   Palmerston & Reed Publishing Co.
1524 S. Big Bend Blvd.
St. Louis, MO 63117
1-877-99-BOOKS (toll free)
www.palmerston.com

Dedications

First and foremost I want to express my thanks and gratitude to Sally Rains for her never-ending enthusiasm and determination for this book. You go, girl!

I'm also grateful to my wife, Anne, for teaching me about nurturing and for all of our work together teaching parenting classes and camps and couples classes over the past 11 years. She has always been there to keep me organized and handle the details.

I want to thank my kids Kelly, T.J., and John for being willing to be a part of old family traditions and for creating new ones as well. I love watching them pass on traditions of kindness and empathy and love to younger campers and friends.

I am also very grateful to my parents and Anne's parents and all of my grandparents and aunts and uncles who were very vested in family and tradition. Some of my fondest memories over the years have to do with homemade raviolis at Christmas, October apple butter cookings, and barbecued eye of the rounds. I hope our kids will pass on this spirit of family to their children some day.

Finally, thanks to Palmerston & Reed for taking a chance on this book. I hope publishing Rains-Jordan books becomes a new tradition for them!

Tim Jordan

To B.J. and Mike the two great joys of my life, and to Rob, the one who adds the sweetness to it. Also to my entire family, you all know who you are, the best anyone could ask for.

Sally Tippett Rains

Table Of Contents

Introduction

From Tim Jordan:

I love the title of this book. I think Sally captured perfect-ly the way many, probably most, parents feel today. The pace of life has increased dramatically since I was growing up in the 50s and 60s. So many technological advances, from computers to CDs to cell phones and microwaves and air travel.

And yet, Americans today are working more hours than previous generations. And despite the glut of infiltration pouring into our lives from books and tapes and television and Internet, parents today are more insecure about their parenting effectiveness than ever before. Parents and kids today feel rushed, pressured, stressed out as never before. And, they feel disconnected. Disconnected from each other; from relatives who live in other cities; from neighbors who spend most of their non-working hours glued to their home entertainment centers and computer screens. Very few families feel grounded, secure, sure of themselves.

This is why this book is so timely and important. It's time we took stock of exactly where we are as families. Have we created a healthy balance between work and home? Are we creating the kind and depth of closeness we want with our children? Are we passing on family rituals that connect our children to their past heritage? Are we taking the time to create new traditions that our children will embrace and carry on to their children? Are we managing the day-to-day challenges of our households in ways that will teach and empower our children for their future? Are we keeping our kids grounded when we are flying by the seats of our pants?

This book contains lots of suggestions to help you answer these questions in a positive way for your family.

Whether you work outside the house or stay at home, are married or a single parent, changed jobs or not, you will find many practical ideas in Keeping Your Kids Grounded When You're Flying By The Seat Of Your Pants that will aid you in keeping your ship afloat in these turbulent waters. We will offer suggestions to help in such common everyday areas as homework and household chores, managing after school activities, simple meal time ideas, handling sick kids, starting a new job or moving, money and marital problems. We will also cover more long term issues such as family meetings, keeping spirituality and traditions alive and well in your home, staying connected to your kids during the teenage years, taking care of you, and creating closeness with your children that will last.

So hop aboard and join us for a relaxing, practical and fun ride. This is not a short-term, make-your-family-perfect-in-10-minutes kind of book. This is a chance to take stock of your family's mental health and state of affairs. It is a chance to remember the important stuff that past generations of families have embraced. It is a chance to learn some new ways to effectively handle the current demands that so intensely push on our families. Our hope and intention is that this book will cause you and your family to pause, slow down and rediscover within yourselves the kinds of feelings and experiences that your kids will benefit from today and remember to cherish years from now. Your children deserve all of this and more, and so do you!

From Sally Tippett Rains:

I started on this book several years ago, after moving around the country because of my husband's job. We kept going into new schools where our sons did not know anybody. My husband and I would be occupied with the business of setting up a new home, working at new jobs, and acclimating ourselves to a new area. We wanted to be sure we kept our family first and that all of the moves did not affect our children in a negative way. There were so many things we tried to do to keep our kids grounded. I noticed other families in similar situations even though they had not moved. There were single parents trying to do the big job of raising children, those who have just had job changes, people low on money, and even a family who was struggling with a teenager for the first time. Everyone is so busy these days, but I know we all want the same thing, and that is to raise our children right. I am not an expert and I certainly do not have a perfect family. In my opinion, you don't have to be perfect, you just have to show your family you love them and do your best.

I was glad to have Tim Jordan receive my ideas with enthusiasm and happy that he wanted to become involved with the project. He *is* an expert in child development and family issues and he has a lot of great ideas to offer in this book. My family has not done everything in this book, and some of the things we have tried have not worked, so we tried something else. Every family is different, and you have to do what works for you. The book is a lighthearted offering of ideas from which you can pick and choose in your own quest to keep your family grounded.

My mom, who I do consider to be an expert, gave me the best advice I've ever gotten in the parenting area and it is this: First of all, you were a couple before you were parents, remember that and keep your relationship special.

And, when we had our first son and were afraid we would not be good parents so she told us this: You are the only parent your child has ever known. He is not expecting anything. If you do your best, whatever you do, you will be the best parent in the world to him.

Chapter 1
Kids Will Be Kids

Remember when you were young and your parents hated your music? It can feel like déja vu for many of us as we struggle with *our* children's music. Some may even be tempted to say "turn that down!" or "that's just noise, the real music was back in my day..." And then there are the issues of body piercing, tattoos, baggy pants and chains, hair, and the many other current ways of expressing oneself. Most parents need only look at their own yearbooks to find similar fashions; you may have even worn the long, stringy hair that is so detestable to some parents today. Many of the issues kids face today are similar to the ones we faced growing up, although kids are facing these issues at a much younger age today. The pressures from the culture, i.e. television, the media, advertising, computers and the Internet, are creating much more intense messages about materialism, how to look and dress and act etc. compared to when we grew up. Kids today are facing some very tough issues at very young ages under intense pressures from all sides and without nearly as much support as most of us received. Let us talk a bit about some important issues that most families face today.

The Electronic Age

Back in the 60s, a kid could watch *Leave It To Beaver* and be perfectly content to be lying on the floor watching television. It was a black and white show. By contrast, a very popular show today is *Home Improvement*, which is in color and features a very famous actor, Tim Allen, as the father. As the show goes from scene to scene, there are graphics and funny little sounds added, presumably to keep your attention, as if the show, itself, would not. There are often guest shots by movie stars and times when the children disrespect the parents (although this show is actually pretty good about portraying a good, grounded family, something rarely seen on television these days) and other distractions from just the straight script of the show. These same kinds of graphics and exciting additions have been added to sports broadcasts. When the FOX network got football it added the high tech graphics and the other networks followed. It seems the powers that be do not even think a child will watch a baseball game anymore without adding fancy graphics to the scoreboard and loud exciting music. Would the children of today watch *Leave It To Beaver* every day or do they need the glamorous stars and high tech graphics and color to keep their interest?

It is just automatically assumed that youngsters want the high tech because it is all around them. Electronic games, hand-held games, and computers are all a part of everyday life to a youngster. Many homes have answering machines, caller ID machines, and fax machines.

While computers and electronic games do occupy children, thus leaving the grown-ups with more time to do the things they need to do, it may not be in the best interest of your youngster to constantly be doing these things. There is a buzz that comes from a computer, the television and the electronic games that can cause stress, even though people may not realize it. Parents would do well to limit time spent on the computer and monitor the use of the Internet. A child who can use the computer well and go online with e-mail and access information on the World Wide Web is a child who will have skills for a lifetime. By comparison, a child who's best friend is the computer is a very sad child. Many children come home to an empty house and the only conversation they get is when they go online. While it can be fun to chat with a friend online, it needs to be kept in balance.

That Loud Music

Let's face it, we all like the music we like. The music issue really does not come up until the child is a little older, usually middle school age. While the children are young and generally do not know any better or cannot make the decision, most parents play their music, which is generally oldies or "classics." As the child gets older, they start hearing their friends' music and want to find the most popular radio stations to listen to.

There are several reasons why a parent might not like a song; usually the music seems like "just noise" to them or the words might be offensive. Take the time to remember a few songs from your childhood. Most of the words were not classic poetry. Trying to come to some common ground with music will help in closing the gap between parents and children. If you occasionally turn on a radio station they like, it will seem as though you are "cool" and maybe even understand them (at least for a few minutes!). You do not want to compromise your own morals, but you should loosen your tie a bit when it comes to the music. Most kids, unless they are listening to satanic music (and if they are you should intervene and explain it to them) are not listening to the words as much as the beat. They are just enjoying the music and usually it is in the background anyway. If kids really wants to listen to some types of music, they will figure out a way to do it. They will use headphones in their bedroom or go to a friend's house. We all know from experience that the more negative energy we put to such issues as music or clothes, the more kids tend to rebel and do more of what we do not like.

Talk to your children about their music. As the prayer of St. Francis says, "Seek first to understand, then to be understood." Listen to why your child likes a certain song or group. Get into their shoes, their world. Sometimes as parents, we can make decisions or assumptions that do not turn out to be true. If *they* feel heard, they are more likely to hear *your* thoughts. If you are concerned about a certain group your son or daughter may be listening to, talk to your children about it. Discuss how sometimes people use drugs and music to alter their minds. Try going with them to a music store. Ask your daughter what she thinks about it. You are opening the lines of communications and you are meeting her on her own turf, the loud music store at the mall.

There are many types of music out today. For parents who are concerned about the lyrics of some of the songs, there are many contemporary Christian groups out there who record rock music but with clean lyrics. There are even Christian rap groups that if you did not listen closely to the words, you would not hear a difference from the rap groups being played on the popular radio stations. It is the job of the parents to offer solutions to problems. Don't just criticize and expect your children to find their own way. Help them along.

Safety Issues

When most of us were kids, we said "good-bye" to our mothers and got on our bikes and rode as far as we wanted to. We arrived home at dark or dinner time. Times have changed and things are different today; parents put more restrictions on their children. First of all, they should not be riding their bicycles without a helmet, and secondly, they should not be riding on unfamiliar streets. When setting limits with your children do what feels right in your heart. Follow the guidelines in chapter two on family meetings in giving your kids input on the boundaries and agreements.

Neighborhoods are changing and we do not always know our neighbors. The same is true about friends from school. How do you know the boy your son wants to spend the night with does not have a father who is a hunter and keeps a loaded gun in the closet? If you are relatively strict with your daughter, how do you know that if you let her spend the night with a girlfriend, the girl's parents may not be home, and they may go out without you knowing about it. One way to find out these things is to get to know your children's friends and their friends' parents. If a friend invites your child over, talk to the parents, find out whether or not they have the same feelings you do about things. If you feel the least bit funny about letting you child go to someone's house, go with your gut feeling and say no.

If you just say "you can't go," chances are you will make your child mad. Telling your kids how you feel allows them not to take it personally. It might not be "no" forever, just not until you get to know the friend and his family better.

One alternative is to plan ahead to do something with your family and include one of your child's friends. Older children like to take their friends along. Go bowling or to the driving range or the batting cages. You can pick the friend up, and then you can drop him off when you are finished.

Now you have to remember that most of the time it will be perfectly fine for your children to spend the night with

It's important to teach safety rules, such as when kids are learning to ride a bike

friends. If it is a relative or a friend whose family you know, it will be a good experience for the child to sleep away from home. This gets them ready for the scout camping trips and times when you will be out of town. It can be a very good experience for a child to spend the night at someone's house.

If your children want to join some other children on the next street to play hockey, for instance, it would be a good idea for you to every once in a while walk over to check it out. You could just act like you are taking a walk, or you could bring a water bottle or snacks for everyone. You can do this without embarrassing your child. This helps you get to be a friendly face to the child's friends and you get to know them, too. They might be looking for a good goalie or an all-time pitcher. It also helps your child to know in the back of their minds that at any time my parents may show up, and this both gives them a sense of security and also provides our adult presence out on the playground or streets.

If you are a busy person, it is a blessing if your child finds a friend or a group of friends to play with. This occupies their time and frees up your own time. Remember, as with the television, computer or any other activity that occupies them, do not use it strictly as a baby-sitter. Check on them every few hours. Have times your children should call you. If your son has a long walk to get to a friend's house, it is a good idea to have him give you a call to let you know he got there safely. He knows you care and you know where he is. If he calls you before he comes home you can go about your work in relative peace knowing where he is and anticipating when he will get home. A nice touch when your children call is to say "thanks for calling, I love you." They may not say it back in front of their friends, but they will appreciate it. At a time when you least expect it, you may get and "I love you" back and that is a wonderful feeling.

Chapter 2
Keeping Your Family First

Family Meetings: Our Favorite Tool

I cannot think of a better, more effective process to incorporate into family life than family meetings. I have been teaching parents about family meetings in a parenting class entitled "Redirecting Children's Behaviors (RCB)" since 1988 and have yet to find a family where parents and kids did not find them invaluable. When your family is flying by the seat of it's pants, it needs a process like family meetings to bring everyone together in a tradition that creates closeness as well as handles agreements to ensure more cooperation.

T.J.

First, let us give you the guidelines for how to run family meetings, then we will fill in the gaps about their value.

Family Meeting Guidelines

Family meetings can be a very successful method of enhancing family cooperation and closeness. Here are some ideas for the format of a family meeting.

1. Hold the meeting once a week at a time when everyone in the family can attend. Keep this time sacred—do not keep changing it at everyone's convenience.

2. Take the phone off the hook so there are no interruptions. This helps your children see how valuable these meetings are to you also.

3. Decisions should be made by family consensus, not majority vote. If an agreement cannot be reached after a discussion, table the decision until the next meeting.

4. Elect a new leader and secretary at each meeting. The leader runs the meeting and calls on members for participation. The leader also chooses the fun activity the family will do together at the end of the meeting. (see #10).

5. Begin the meeting with compliments to each family member. Use words like, "I love you because…" or "I'm grateful for you because…" "What I love about you is." Also, you can add "what I love about myself is…" at the end of your turn. Teach children to say thank you after they receive a compliment. Each person will give one acknowledgment to every family member and in turn receive one acknowledgment from each person.

6. Consider keeping an "agenda" list on the refrigerator of items to be discussed at the family meeting time. As problems come up during the week, write them down to be discussed at family meetings.

7. Go on to problem solving. Does anyone have a problem they would like to bring up? Listen to anyone's complaints or concerns, then encourage them to suggest a solution. Teach your children that if they complain, it is helpful to think of a solution. A person who is not a part of the solution is part of the problem. Brainstorm as a family, acknowledge each person's ideas and create a win-win situation that works for everyone.

The key to communication is to acknowledge one another.

8. Include a review of the next week's calendar and plan some activities together as a family.

9. For more productive meetings, sit at a cleared table and chairs versus family room. Do not have this meeting during mealtime.

10. Always end the meeting by having the leader choose a fun activity that the whole family can do together.

11. Never force anyone to attend the meetings. If your children do not attend the meetings, check to see why. Check in with yourself to make sure there is nothing you are doing or not doing that would make the meetings more safe, fun, and inviting for everyone.

12. Make an agreement with each other that if someone does not attend the meeting, that person still needs to abide by the agreements that were made at the meeting.

13. Meetings should last no more than 20-40 minutes depending on your children's ages.

(These guidelines were adapted by Tim and Anne Jordan from the book Positive Parenting by Jane Nelson, ED.D and have been used in the parenting course Redirecting Children's Behavior by Kath Kvols.)

Comments

Acknowledging each other at the start of the meeting sets the tone. Kids, teens and parents all love to be acknowledged by their loved ones. Kids get to practice *giving* acknowledgments and *receiving* them. Think of how tough it is for many adults today to receive praise or encouragement. Regular family meetings will allow our kids to easily take in nurturing and encouragement from their family and friends. We would also suggest that for your first two meetings, just do the acknowledgments, the activity planning, and the fun game together. Children then understand that these meetings are not just gripe sessions or for crisis management. They are fun, encouraging and empowering.

It may take some time and patience and practice for your family to learn how to create win-win agreements and to gain consensus. But what a gift for your children to be able to acquire this skill! Just think how empowering it can be for the youngest child to be able to voice a concern and be heard and validated, and then be able to have just as much input on the final agreement as their parents or older siblings. Parents should set the tone by getting everyone to agree that there will be no "put downs" or criticisms during the meetings. This allows everyone to feel safe and let it all hang out.

The more input that children have with the solutions or agreements about chores, bedtime, television, etc. and the more buy-in they experience, more cooperation follows. The family then holds each other accountable to the agreements. It is no longer the king and queen handing down edicts. It is a democracy, with shared responsibility and power. If people start slacking off on the agreements, you can bring it up at the next meeting and work out the kinks. Isn't it a lot more reasonable and tolerable to discuss chores every 3 or 4 months versus dealing with *daily* power struggles? You bet it is!

When your family is flying by the seat of their pants it is easy for family members to feel disconnected from each other; to feel like their opinions do not count and that they are not heard. A lot of the mischief between siblings and around routines like homework and bedtime and chores is due to children feeling discouraged, disconnected from parents and not valuable or powerful. Weekly family meetings will handle all of these areas. It only requires 20-40 minutes each week, which even the busiest of families can find time for. If you are a single parent, then it is just perfect for a meeting to involve just you and one child. Teenagers may grouse at first at how "weird" it sounds, but I've never had a family yet that did not report back after a handful of meetings that their teens loved the meetings and are the first ones to remind the parents about the next one.

The same goes for blended families. What better way to gain cooperation with kids who live in two different homes with two different sets of parents and siblings? Both households can hold meetings so that everyone is clear about agreements and expectations (which may differ between the two places). It allows kids a safe place to voice concerns about stepparents and for stepparents to clarify their role in issues such as discipline with their stepchildren. Being up front and clear about agreements is an absolute necessity when dealing with blended families. Family meetings can meet these needs effectively.

Chapter 3
Your Goodwill Account

As a bank account provides us with information about
the relationship between our deposits and withdrawals and
the state of our finances, so a Goodwill Account represents
the relationship between ourselves and our children—our
deposits, withdrawals, and the state of our relationship
afterward. The goodwill account provides the foundation
from which everything in your family will flow.

How is your relationship with your children? How does
it feel? What does it look like? If the account is full, because
you have made lots of deposits, then the relationship will
feel safe, respectful, close, loving, warm, trusting, and
accepting.

If A Goodwill Account is Full,
Children and Parents Are More Willing To:

Listen to each other
Hear the other person's side or point of view
Cooperate
Pitch in when things need to be done
Be more flexible
Apologize when they were wrong
Trust each other
Be held accountable
Express their feelings honestly and directly to the person involved
Tell the truth
Own up to and take responsibility for their mistakes
Sit down together and create win-win agreements
Show their love and affection for each other
Encourage and support each other.

Though it sounds like Camelot, most parents have as their goal raising healthy, grounded kids in a loving, nurturing family. The following are some examples of how you can start making regular deposits to achieve those goals.

Respect

This is true for all ages, and especially during the adolescent years when teens are very sensitive to being disrespected by adults. Respect can look like not judging them by their external appearance, seeing things from their point of view, not yelling at them and using their ideas in agreements (see chapter on family meetings.)

It means treating them with the same respect you would show to your best friend. You would allow your friend to say no to you, wouldn't you? You would hold your best friend accountable to agreements? You would not keep double standards with your best friend, yet we do it all the time with the kids. "There is no yelling in this house!" we scream. Another example would be lecturing them about not drinking and especially not drinking and driving, yet when a parent drinks a glass of wine before heading out of the house and into the driver's seat it creates a double standard.

Respect can also look like honoring a child's personality, temperament, and developmental level.

When our son, John was four years old, we would take him to church with books, coloring books and crayons in tow. He would be fine for about 15-20 minutes (his limit on sitting still) sitting quietly in a place not the least bit designed for his needs. When we noticed his voice getting a bit louder and he was starting to drop things "accidentally" under the seat, I would walk him outside for five to ten minutes, where we would look at the leaves and talk out loud. After he blew off a little steam, we would head back into the church where he could handle the last 20 minutes. By respecting his need for a break and handling it before he would lose it, we avoided a power struggle and a scene. In the process, we made a deposit into the goodwill account.

T.J.

Dates

One-on-one time, especially when you take your child outside the house is a great deposit into your good will account. Kids feel special, loved and close. As we mentioned previously, "dates" with your child can be a very special time. They can be anything from playing in the park to going to a movie.

My son, John, and I hike to our special hideaway cliff in the woods where we might eat lunch, throw rocks in the creek and chase frogs. I started a tradition of taking my kids out to breakfast before school many years ago. My sons, TJ and John would go to a local restaurant where they traditionally ordered a hot chocolate with an extra bowl of whipped cream on the side. We would sit at the same table, order the same breakfast, play the same games of tic-tac-toe and hangman until the meal came. My daughter Kelly and I have been going to a used paperback bookstore for years. Different dates for different children make each of them feel special. These special times are helping me to make deposits in their accounts. It is often during these one on one times that we have our best discussions, free from all of the disruptions at home.

T.J.

You can learn a lot about what's going on with your kids on these special dates. It is good for the parent, also, because you are free from the disruptions you always have. Plan the dates with your child so they can look forward to it. Put it on the calendar, and never, ever (ever!) forget them or cancel out.

Our good friends and fellow authors, Linda and Richard Eyre, whose books include Teaching Your Children Values and Teaching Your Children Responsibility also advocate making dates with your children even if you have a lot of them. They have nine children yet they both schedule times with each child alone. At various stages in their lives the children were of different ages and some have married and moved out, but they wanted to be sure to know each child on an individual basis and felt it was important to the child to feel he or she was special to both parents. At family meetings they discussed the dates and then planned on a calendar when each child's special day would be. If it was Linda's turn to take out their daughter, Charity, for example, the two would discuss where they wanted to go. This gave both of them something fun to look forward to and it teaches the children the value of their family.

S.T.R.

Going on a "date" is a good way to spend time with your children.

Since it is assumed that if you are reading this, you have limited time, you might be thinking 'how would I have time to make special time with each of my children?' Special time can be as simple as stopping for a snow cone on the way home from dancing lessons or going out for a fast food breakfast before dropping your child off at school. We are not talking about long involved things. The important thing is show your children they are worth spending a little time on.

Saturday morning is a great time to make a date with your child or teenager. You can go out to breakfast, and maybe do an errand on the way home. This allows your spouse to sleep in, and you can enjoy special time with your child. If there are other youngsters at home, your spouse can enjoy special time with them, also. The errand may be as simple as getting the child a much needed haircut. The idea of taking them out and making them feel special will appeal to your child, and you can also accomplish something you needed to get done at the same time.

Give More Power, Say-So, and Control

Giving your children more power by giving them choices and decision making opportunities is another way to make deposits in the account. Let your children teach you something like a song, or a dance, or how to play one of their electronic games. Allow them to stretch and meet challenges. Teach them how to do their own wash or cut the grass or balance your check book for you. Family meetings are a great place to give kids say-so about their everyday life. There are literally hundreds of opportunities every day to turn over more decision making or power to your kids. Make a conscious effort and the opportunities will appear as if by magic.

Apologize when you are wrong

If you make a mistake or if you are wrong about something, there is nothing wrong with owning up to it and apologizing. In fact, there is something very right about it. This is a very powerful deposit into your goodwill account. It conveys a lot of respect for the other person.

I remember when our son, TJ, was about four or five years old, I spanked him for the first and last time. He was dragging his feet in getting ready for church one Sunday morning. He had a large container of crayons under his arm. I asked him to just take a few crayons in a sandwich bag and he refused.

When I came back a few minutes later he again refused to not take the big crayon box, throwing them down and yelling something at me. I just lost it and as he ran by me I popped his rear end and he yelled again and ran upstairs to his room. Halfway up the stairs I caught myself. I stopped and took a moment to cool off. When I went into his room he was laying face down on his bed crying, which made me feel even worse. I sat beside him and rubbed his back for a moment, apologizing about ten times for spanking him. He turned and said to me,

It's important to apologize to your kids when you're wrong.

"that's not the worse part, I was so shocked and scared running up the stairs that I peed in my pants!" Well, he might as well have stuck a dagger in my heart. I could not have felt worse. He changed clothes, we drove to church, and as we were entering the building I stopped and asked him to take a walk with me. We went over to a swingset, swung for a moment, and then I apologized again, telling how bad I felt. I told him that I remember my parents yelling at us as kids and being spanked and how I had sworn to myself that I would never do that to my kids. I committed to him that it would never happen again, which 10 years later still holds true. I think I turned a withdrawal into a deposit with my apology.

T.J.

Unconditional Love

I know this deposit seems so obvious, but in this hustle bustle busy world, many kids feel disconnected. There are many preschool children who leave their homes at 6:30 a.m. five days a week and do not arrive home until after 5:30 p.m. Their parents are usually tired. Many end up becoming distracted by looking at their mail, checking the answering machine for messages, flipping on the news or scurrying around the kitchen trying to find something to throw together for dinner (see chapter on meals).

Parents who work outside the home should drop everything when they get home, put on some play clothes and spend some uninterrupted time playing with their kids. Run around, kick soccer balls, play loud music and dance, or maybe curl up with them on your lap in a rocker and read stories. In some way, re-connect with your child. You both need it and deserve it after a long day apart. That special time together gives everyone a chance to feel loved and connected, and it gives everyone a chance to let the hassles of the day melt away. It also sets a warm tone for the rest of the evening as well. This type of 20-30 minute deposit will pay huge dividends.

Do not forget about bedtime. Reading books while snuggled under the covers is a great way to love each other at the end of the day. Ask them questions about their happiest or saddest moment of the day. Talk about what they are most proud of, and tell them what you love about them.

My son, TJ, who is 14-years-old, will ask his mom to rub his feet with some peppermint foot massage cream. She will haul her tired body up to his top bunk and grant his wish. While she is massaging his feet, he will talk about this day or whatever is on his mind.

T.J.

Look for ways to have these special connections. Kids can directly feel and experience our love for them during these times.

There are many more ways to make deposits into your goodwill account with your children, but there are also ways that if you are not careful, you could be making *withdrawals*. Withdrawals would be anything that causes kids to feel more distant, disrespected, unloved, hurt or unsafe. Withdrawals could be things like yelling at them, spanking them, calling them names, being sarcastic, invalidating or dismissing their feelings, not being fully present with them (distracted), criticizing or judging them, being stuck in a punishment cycle with them; withdrawing our love because we are angry or hurt.. If the withdrawals outnumber the deposits and the goodwill account gets low, the relationship feels very unsafe and distant. There is usually a lot of mischief going on on both sides. Revenge, getting even and being right become more important than closeness.

Looking at it from their point of view, it is nearly impossible to create cooperation or to sit down in good faith and create win-win agreements because there is no good faith left. It is hard to hold kids accountable because of this lack of a relationship. They do not care anymore because they do not feel cared for. They feel disconnected and unloved.

The first and most important step in turning things around is to start making deposits into the account. Hold off on the agreements until the goodwill account is fuller. Only then will the cooperation be possible.

Obviously the best bet is prevention; so even if you and your family are flying by the seat of your pants, put making deposits into your goodwill account at the top of your list of to-dos. Remember that everything flows from the relationship. If it is close, safe and respectful, then things get done and agreements are kept. If you happen to hit a bump, people are flexible and understanding, and more willing to pitch in until things are back on track. If the account is low, then bumps become mountains that seem unsurpassable.

Adding to your goodwill account becomes routine after a while. It just becomes the way your family does business. It becomes a part of your fabric. Remember to work (or should we say 'play') on your deposits. If you do you will enjoy the short and long term dividends for the rest of your family's journey.

Chapter 4
Making Time For Your Kids
On The Busiest of Days

Eat As Many Meals Together As Possible (See next chapter for tips on easy meals)

As your family starts going in different directions, the traditional family dinner table can easily get left behind. If your family shared dinners at the end of the day on a regular basis when you were young, you probably have a warm feeling about these and the conversations that occurred around the table. You will carry these memories with you forever, and your children deserve to continue in that tradition.

Get the children involved in the dinner experience. Your hectic schedule may prevent you from making those home-cooked meals that your mother or grandmother may have made, but it is not the food that is important here. The thing that counts is the fellowship and ritual of sitting down for dinner.

Try to make dinner interesting and different. Sometimes that little extra touch will make the kids want to come to dinner. Try using candles, table cloths, centerpieces at least every other week. It does not matter if you use china or paper plates, candles can set a warm and comfortable mood. You will not be hearing, "I'll be there in a minute, I'm watching my favorite show," if you use candles. You will hear, "Can I light the candles tonight?" The beauty of the candles and table cloth is that they can make a tuna casserole or take-out Chinese food feel like a meal you worked hard on.

On candle night, it is "restaurant behavior" night. Have the children put their napkin (or paper towel!) on their lap. You should do it also. Stress manners and if you do this on a regular basis, you will have children who will do fine when you go out to eat or eat at someone else's house.

Children like to help set the dinner table with you if you make it sound fun. Try to make sure their playmates go home or stay outside during dinner. This should be family time, and it is hard to have good quality family discussions when the neighbor kid is watching your television in the next room. It is hard to send your children's friends home sometimes, but it is important to reserve some time for the family even if it seems like the children do not like the idea at the time.

Remember that dinner may be the best, and only, time you really get to talk to your children. Go around the table and have each person tell what they did today. Another conversation starter is to have each person tell one thing they learned today. We all learn something every day, but often do not think about it. School children learn something every day, but if you ask them "What did you at school today?"

you will probably get an answer like "nothing," or "went to gym," "ate lunch, had a snack." If you make them think about what they learned, you will start a conversation and they will also be going over things they learned, thus making them remember it better.

The grown-ups should also be included in this "What did you learn today" game. If you can not think of anything you learned, capitalize on what your children are learning and say, "I learned that the capital of Bolivia is La Paz, from Bobby, just now. I really learned that when I was your age, but I had forgotten. What else did you learn about Bolivia, Bobby?" This encourages your children to talk to you.

Limit Television

The television can be your family's best friend or its arch enemy, depending on how you use it. It may sound cliché to say you should limit your children's time in front of the tube, but it is so important. If you are going to limit their television time, know that you are committing yourself to less TV as well.

Busy parents often let the television serve as a baby-sitter, which can be fine if you need to be doing something. If you get into this habit on a regular basis, your kids will automatically turn the television on whenever they come home. The constant chatter and noise from the television in the background is so common in American homes that sometimes it is not even noticed.

At a family meeting, bring up your concerns that everybody, parents included, are watching too much television and ask them what they think would be a reasonable amount of tube time. Negotiate it, and come to a family consensus. The times may differ for school nights versus weekends versus summer time. By giving them a lot of input, you will get more cooperation. Use that newly liberated free time to spend time together playing cards or board games or four square or reading.

Encourage the children to go outside to play or read or play a game if they say there is nothing to do. Have them write a letter to a grandparent, aunt or uncle or someone who has been nice to them. Letter writing is beginning to become a lost art and all it takes is a few short minutes once the child learns to write.

Read With Your Children

Even if your children can read themselves or seem a little to old for it, they will treasure the times you spend reading to them. Reading with great enthusiasm will also instill in them an interest in books. For toddlers, you can read easy to read books and point to the words as you read. Older children will enjoy hearing adventure stories or even magazine or newspaper articles. If you have not found the time to read that *Sports Illustrated* article you wanted to read, gather your children around and read it to them. It accomplishes two things at once: time with your children and time for the things you want to do. It may even bring you closer to your kids by developing common interests.

No matter how old they are, children love it when you read to them.

You might even want to pick up one of the older classics to read to them. These are books they might not otherwise read because they are too young or they do not seem as interesting as *Star Wars*. You would be surprised at how quickly you can get through even thick books by reading one chapter each night. Books like *Treasure Island* or *Robinson Crusoe* are fun to read together. Read the real ones too, not the abridged versions. What a great way to open your kids' minds to adventures and characters that have been read for generations.

Besides reading to them, you should try to have a little time for them to read to you. Some creative ways to make sure your kids read to you each day are having them read in the car on the way home from school, to or from lessons, or on a trip to the grocery store. If you have to work and have absolutely no time in your schedule at home, call them from work and have them read to you over the phone.

Another good way to instill reading into children is for you to read. If you are reading a book, you can say to your child, "let's have D.E.A.R. time," which means "Drop Everything And Read." You both sit down and read quietly to yourselves. Sometimes it is more fun if it is warm outside to set up a blanket under a tree and read outdoors. Set a time limit, even 15 minutes is good and it gets you both in the habit of reading.

For those times you are away, tape yourself reading stories and let them listen to the tapes before bedtime or during breakfast. They will feel close to you when they hear your voice.

Leave Your Children Notes

Tucking a special note away is an easy thing to do, and it is something that just lets your children know you are thinking of them and that you love them. Notes in their lunch box are a nice surprise. Notes in their math book or history book will bring a welcome smile during a boring lecture. Imagine how encouraging a note that says "Good luck on your spelling test, you can do it!" would be right before a test.

You will want to make sure the notes are private between you and your child because as they get older it could be embarrassing to have their friends see a note from their mother or father at the wrong time or in the wrong place. They know your writing, you can leave a note and leave it unsigned if that is a concern with a junior high or high school student.

Note writing is also a nice touch with your spouse. Actually, most of the ideas here could be adapted to increase togetherness with couples, also. It may not seem like much, but little things that show you care and are thinking about each other mean so much. You are never too old to enjoy a little surprise. It is fun to find an "I love you" on the bathroom mirror (written in lipstick or shaving cream?) or a "Good luck with your presentation" in a briefcase, or a "We miss you" tucked in an overnight bag.

If someone writes you a note back, show your appreciation by displaying it in a personal way. A little yellow sticky note that says "I love you" will cheer you up if you put it up by your desk or on the refrigerator. It will also encourage the note writer to do it again.

Do Projects With Your Children

Depending on what kind of person you are, pick something you can handle. Some people do crafts, others cook, others do difficult kinds of exercises. There are so many things you can do with your children. Try to find things they would enjoy doing. It may require getting down to their level and playing with them. One simple thing is to make playing dough and sit down with your child and create.

Directions for making playing dough
  1 cup flour
  1/2 cup salt
  1/2 cut water
  1/2 teaspoon salad oil

Mix the ingredients. It gets harder as you knead it. You can put food coloring in it, but it's easier and less messy if you just use it the way it is.

Try to include the kids in your hobbies and projects.

The kids enjoy it so much they do not even notice it is white. It is so easy and quick but it makes your child see that you do things that interest them and you can have fun doing them, too. It is the perfect antidote to their boredom, and it also allows you some special one-on-one time with them.

Holidays or changing seasons are a great way to get your children to do crafts.

Valentines Mailbox
Get a large piece of white construction paper. Fold in half and staple the two sides. It will form a pocket. Now you have a "Valentine's Mailbox". Give the kids some red construction paper and show them how to cut out hearts. Another version of a Valentines Mailbox is covering a shoe box with white paper and decorating it. The whole point is

to make a mailbox and then that leads to making valentines. If you decide you want to make a Valentine's Mailbox or any other craft, you do not have to have a lot of time to do it. For example, begin making the Valentines Mailbox and after you have stapled the sides, have the kids cut out red hearts. This may take a while so you could put it all in a paper bag to finish the next day. After the hearts are cut out, you can glue them on and if there is a little more time left, you can give the child some crayons to decorate the pocket.

Make A Friendship Bracelet

Another great crafty idea is friendship bracelets. Have the children pick out the yarn colors they like at a craft store. The simplest kind of bracelet is made by using three strands of heavy yarn and braiding them together, like girls braid their hair. Hold the three strands the right one goes over the middle one, the left one goes over the middle one, the right one goes over the middle one, and so on. Many kids already know how to make them and *they* can teach *you* how to make the different varieties. There are some neat how-to books at craft stores to get you going. These bracelets make cool gifts, plus they wake up the creative little kid in all of us.

Crafts are a great thing to do with your kids. It really takes no talent at all to have a craft box available. Keep markers, crayons, colored construction paper and other little knick knacks in it and pull it out whenever you need it.

Craft Box Essentials

Crayons, construction paper, markers, scissors, glue, stick-on stars, tape, stickers, popsicle sticks, brads, paper plates, yarn, tissue paper

Sharing what little time you have with your kids means so much to them. There are other projects you can do with your kids. Do you need something sanded? Have your child sand it a little. How about planting a garden? They just love getting out there in the dirt.

Sometimes you feel so swamped that you think you have absolutely no time to do "projects" with your kids. You have laundry to do, right? Play "The Laundry Sorting Game."

The Laundry Sorting Game

Divide the laundry into categories with your child or children (I'll take the socks and underwear, you take the towels and shirts). Say "go" and whoever gets theirs folded neatly first is the winner. This accomplishes two goals, again, being with your child and getting the laundry folded.

The earlier your children get introduced to doing the laundry, the more well-rounded they will be.

What about cooking? You have to fix dinner, right? Even if you are in a big hurry to get to that PTA meeting, you have to fix dinner. Have one child read the directions and the other one do it. It makes a child feel important and valuable to have you say, "Cindy made the dinner," or "David made the soup." Everyone loves to be valuable so it makes them want to help peel the carrots, set the table or just turn the microwave on. Provide your kids lots of opportunities to feel valuable in ways that contribute to the overall management of your home.

Besides making the dinner, a child can be in the same room with you while you are cooking and be doing something else. If you are planning a party and have a lot of work to do, why not try teaching your children the "Polish The Silver Game."

Polish The Silver Game

Get out your tarnished silver and your polishing cloth and silver cleaner. Show your child how much fun it is to see a blackened area turn to bright silver just by rubbing. After the child gets excited about it, hand over the cloth and say, "now you can try it." If there are two children, divide up the dishes and see who can polish their pile first.

After your children sees the progress being made by polishing the silver, they will become more enthusiastic. It is like magic the way the bowl starts out tarnished and dull and the harder they rub it, the shinier it gets. This one can work well and you can even include the neighbor kids, it looks so fun.

Play With Your Kids

This is probably one of the most important things in keeping your kids grounded in a busy world. Let them know you truly enjoy their company and take a special notice in them. It takes maybe ten minutes to play a game of catch with your child, but it is worth it. There are always an extra ten minutes in your life if you choose to take them. Do it while you are waiting for dinner to cook. Do it while you are waiting for the school bus. Do it before you take them to youth league games. A simple game of catch can be so rewarding. The words "playing catch" can be substituted with shooting hoops, throwing the football, playing chopsticks together on the piano,

Sometimes to play with a kid, act like a kid

dancing to a new song, whatever, but do it with your kids. Even if you are not a good athlete your child will appreciate the time you play with him.

Make A Batting Tee
Here is a fun way to show your interest in your child, while teaching them the value of working on a project. Baseball and softball players of all ages can benefit by using a batting tee. It's not just for tee ball. Wendell Kim, the third base coach for the Boston Red Sox in his book Youth Baseball, A Coach's and Parent's Guide says, " tees have been found to be a very important tool in developing a level swing. Accordingly, ballplayers of all ages can and should practice with tees." Help your child make a batting tee, and then get out there with the child and work on that level swing.

Materials needed:
* Wooden base (scrap plywood works well) approximately 1 1/2 square feet.
* One foot of radiator hose or other similar rubber tubing
* Wooden dowel rod (1 1/2" in diameter – should allow the radiator hose to slip over it)
* Four 2" corner braces
* Sixteen 3/4" Phillips wood screws
* Saw

Directions:
    First decide how tall the batting tee needs to be by determining the strike zone of the person for whom it is being made. Saw the pole a little shorter than the actual size needed. Slide the hose down on top of the rod.
    Next, cut the wood in the shape of home plate or just keep it square. Attach the brackets to the dowel rod with the

screws and then screw it into the base.

Now Practice!

Set the baseball on top of the tee and practice swinging. If it is too tall, the radiator hose can be removed and the dowel rod can be cut. Help your child to practice his or her swing step by step. The more times you swing the bat, the more your body gets used to a certain way of doing it. The drill of practicing your swing is something that players of all ages need to do.

Caution:

This is a portable batting tee, and a fragile one at that. It was designed to show you how you can make simple things with your children which require not much time or money. If you take a huge swing, be prepared to chase your batting tee down. The radiator hose gives it flexibility, but nothing guarantees that if you make a bad swing and hit the center of the pole, you will not knock it over. It is just a fun activity and helps your child see that you are coming into his world and helping him with something he is interested in.

Puzzles Are Fun

Do things they like to do. A puzzle is a good thing to set up in an out of the way place. Whenever you have a few spare minutes, you can work on the puzzle together. If you are waiting for the baby-sitter, work on the puzzle. After you are gone your child can feel like you are with them as they work on the puzzle to show you when you return. Do not forget to notice how much your child completed while you were gone.

Watch Family Videos or Look At Scrapbooks

It only takes a few minutes between activities to turn on the video and pop in a tape. Your children will enjoy watching videos of when they were "little." Sitting with your children and watching yourselves on happy occasions reinforces how important your family is to each other. If you do not have a video camera, try to keep scrapbooks, or at least put the pictures in one central box. The reason you saved the pictures was so you could look back on that fun time, so do not forget to do that.

Wonderful family discussions or one-on-one talks can develop when you are looking at family pictures. It is also fun for your children to look at some pictures of you when you were a child. You will want to watch their reaction because you do not want to bore them with your pictures. Showing them what you were like and talking about what you did when you were younger can bring on good conversations.

Give Them Chores And Responsibilities

Every day there should be certain "chores" that should be expected (See chapter five on household chores). The chores should be age appropriate and simple for younger children. Make the bed, set out your clothes the night before, put their laundry where it goes, comb your hair, wash your face, brush your teeth and get dressed for the day could be the chores. Older children could take out the trash, empty the dishwasher, take care of the dog, fold the clothes, or even do their own wash. If you have to do all these things for your children, you are going to have hectic mornings. If you teach them to do for themselves and then come to you for inspection, you will give them a reason to be proud of themselves.

Now you may have to live with lumpy beds, mismatched clothes or toothpaste in the sink, but if you can let these things go, it makes for a smoother morning.

It is also helpful to set out the cereal bowls spoons and

toaster and let the children (over five) get their own breakfast with you checking in on them. They love it when you can sit down and eat with them. If they can get their own food together, you will have time to get ready. If you have time, try to eat it with them and talk to them. Some kids like adults are not "morning people." Just your presence at the breakfast table gives them the message that you care and are there for them if they need you or have something to say. Put that newspaper down, they deserve your undivided attention.

Homework is a chore and children should have a routine as to when and where they do it. (See chapter five on homework) Make sure you take time to go over their homework and be interested in it. Check backpacks and call homework hotlines if they have them. Being involved in your children's schoolwork is rewarding because it spawns conversations. "How was your math test?" "What are your spelling words?" "What was the field trip like?"

Give Your Children A Spiritual Foundation

No matter what your religious beliefs are, you need to have a spiritual foundation and share it with your children (See chapter 16 on religion). Throughout a child's life and into adolescence and adulthood, a strong religious foundation can be one of the most important ingredients in a stable grounded person.

Religious holidays are the easiest way to explain your beliefs to a child. A more detailed explanation of ways to give your children a spiritual foundation can be found in chapter 16.

Give Them A Pat On The Back

Touching your children can give them a feeling of security and love. Take every opportunity to give hugs, kisses and say "I love you." If you are not a "huggy" person, maybe now is the time to start. Besides the touches, develop secret signals, winks, smiles and waves so that when you see your child in a crowd you can greet him or her in a spe-- cial way that says, "I love you."

Try very hard to see good in your child even when it's difficult. On report card day, take the time to really look at the report card. Avoid the tendency to just glance at it in the hustle and bustle of the daily routine and then blurt out your disapproval for fallen grades. If you look closely at a report card and you see a grade that has gone down, if you keep looking, you will probably see one that went up or at least stayed the same. Ask your child what *they* think about their grades and you will usually get an honest and accurate answer. Ask them what they could do differently next semester if any grade is a disappointment. Mirror back their pride in successes, large or small. Build in celebrations like going out to dinner at the end of each quarter no matter what the report card shows. The purpose for the dinner is a traditional time to go out together and celebrate their efforts, not so much the results.

Take every opportunity to say "I love you" to your children.

Making Sure The Kids Don't Feel Left Out In a Family Crisis

It is important to try to make your kids feel grounded every day but sometimes circumstances come along that you just can't plan for. An example of this would be a grandparent's death, sudden loss of a job, or injury. Try to include the children whenever possible, but sometimes you should contact your pediatrician to ask for guidance.

My husband's father died suddenly when he was four and his brother was six. Different friends and family members tried to tell my mother-in-law to bring the children to their father's funeral. Some people told her not to. Luckily for her, their pediatrician called her and advised her not to involve them in the actual funeral or burial. Because she talked to a professional she felt good about her decision, and she has always known in her heart she did the right thing.

S.T.R.

There are several things you can do with your children to help them get through the time when a grandparent dies. Look at pictures of the person in younger days. Talk about memories you had with them. Reassure your children that you take steps to make sure you will live a long healthy live (and make sure you do them).

The loss of an older relative gives you the chance to explain that that is the way life goes. If other relatives come into town or get together, it is a good thing to take advantage of them by helping the children to get to know their relatives. This helps them know how everyone fits in in a family.

Chapter 5
Spend Less Time In The Kitchen
And More Time With Your Children

Dinnertime is a necessity because we all have to eat. When our everyday lives become so hectic that dinnertime becomes so fast and furious that it evolves into fast food or grab what you can, you need to get a grip. There are a lot of creative ways you can accomplish the task of just feeding everyone, but at the same time having a little family time so you can continue in your quest to keep your family grounded and stable. Meals together are important to good healthy family lives, but with all of the lessons and games and meetings that go on, it is often hard to achieve the "traditional family meal." We offer a few ideas for making your life a little easier in the kitchen, and in turn spending more time with your kids.

Some Fun Things To Make With The Whole Family

These are fun meals or food that you can all do together. One other advantage to getting your kids involved in the cooking process is that they take ownership in the meal and are more apt to eat it. They take pride in what they made and it gives them a sense of accomplishment.

Bar-B-Q Pizzas
Ingredients:
Bread dough for the crust (Can be instant baking mix, pizza dough, bread dough or biscuit dough)

Sauce (Choose pizza sauce, vegetarian tomato sauce, barbecue sauce, salsa)

Meat or Vegetable Toppings (Suggestions: chicken, beef, hamburger, sausage, green pepper, onions, mushrooms, tomatoes, grated cheese (any type), bacon bits)

Aluminum foil

Brown the meat in a pan and have all of the toppings ready when the coals are. Set up a table next to the grill with all of the toppings on it. Lay the aluminum foil across the grate on the barbecue grill. Spray it with non-stick spray. Have everyone wash their hands and then give them a ball of dough. Each person can pat out his or her own pizza dough and set it on the fire. Close the lid and keep checking on it. (We burned a few when we first started making these because it's hard to gauge, so you may want to just try one at first -S.T.R.). When you can flip the pizza crust to the other side, it is time for the fun. Everyone grabs from the toppings and puts them on their own pizzas. Sometimes the pizza crusts will break when you turn them over, so you just have to be flexible. A broken piece of pizza crust tastes just the same with all the toppings dumped on it. After everyone gets their toppings on, close the lid for just a short period of time. (Enough time for everyone to fix their drinks and get a plate and fork) Open it up, take the aluminum foil out and put it on a tray or cookie sheet. Set it all on the table and you and your family can enjoy a meal you all had fun making.

Green Cookies (also known as Spinach Balls)
    Make these with your children some Saturday, and then freeze them. Kids will enjoy getting all gooey when they make these. Pop them out of the freezer and into the oven or microwave for a very healthy snack (or a great hors d'oeurve if guests drop by).
Ingredients:
2 10 oz. pkg. frozen chopped spinach, cooked and drained
3 cups herb-seasoned stuffing mix
1 large onion chopped
6 eggs beaten
3/4 cup melted butter
1/2 cup parmesan cheese
1/2 tablespoon pepper
1 1/2 teaspoon salt
1/2 teaspoon thyme or oregano

Mix the ingredients with a large spoon and cool it down in the refrigerator. After a few hours, or overnight, shape it into 3/4" balls. This is the fun part to do with kids of all ages. If you start them very young, they will always like them even when they find out it's "spinach." Cook at 325° for 15-20 minutes. Makes 11 dozen and they are great to freeze in small portions in separate bags and pull them out when needed.

Other Creative Ideas To Give You More Time With Your Kids And Less Time Cooking

Dinner Game Night

Dinner Game Night is a fun way to get your family to sit down together for dinner. One of the problems involved in corralling the family to sit down is getting them all there at the same time--prefer-ably while the food is still hot. Have you ever prepared a meal and called, "Dinner's ready!" only to hear "In a minute!" "There's only 5 minutes to go in this show" or "What are we having?" The object of Dinner Game Night is to give them something to look forward to and be enthusiastic about.

For a special night, playing a game along with dinner can be fun.

Pick a fun, easy to prepare meal. To make it easier pre-pare it in the morning. A "Submarine Sandwich" would be a good choice (see below). Another fun thing would be to have the kids make something after school, like fresh salsa to eat with some chips at dinner. This gets them anticipating the meal.

Set the table and get the game out. If you do it earlier in the game, it "advertises" the fun dinner and gives way to antic-ipation. After putting the plates and silverware on, set the game box out as a decoration and pass out what is needed.

Some good games for game night: Jeopardy, Password,

Wheel of Fortune, Board Games (take up a little more room, but are fun), Trivial Pursuit (regular and junior version together), Disney Trivia Game, Candy Land and Chutes and Ladders.

The games without boards work better for a smaller table. Card games are too much trouble because they require holding the cards.

When the kids see the table all fixed up with the games—and possibly some other festive decoration if you are so inclined—they will look forward to dinner.

At dinnertime, call them and watch them come running. First remember to say grace and ask what everyone's been doing that day so as to have some family conversation. Then, explain what is going on.

"This is a special night, we're going to play a game while we eat dinner. Here are the rules."

It is important the parent explains the rules so everybody will know how to play. If it is a success, you could try it at a later date with an older child planning the game. Remember, you are trying to have fun so encourage leniency in their answers and emphasize the fun camaraderie rather than the competition of the game.

Dinner Game Night is a good thing to do when there have been a lot of sports, lessons, play practices or other distractions and the family dinner has had to suffer recently.

Submarine Sandwiches (One type)

Take a loaf of French bread and slice it down the middle. Add whatever your family likes: cheese, turkey, beef, lunch meat, tomatoes, onions, lettuce, etc. A nice dressing makes it taste better and pre-prepared salad dressings and submarine sandwich dressings can be purchased a the grocery store. Sprinkle a little on the bread before you begin building the sandwich. As you put on the tomatoes or other veggies, sprinkle a little more dressing on. After making the sandwich put it in a plastic bag and store in the refrigerator.

Grocery Services

There are companies who will deliver your groceries to you. Some people use the delivery services that their local grocery stores provide. Others use the frozen food delivery services. These can be more expensive, but then the benefit is that you save time from shopping and are able to spend more time with your children. The frozen delivery services provide quick and easy dinners which go from freezer to stove or microwave in less than half an hour.

On-Line Grocery Shopping

The 21st century has arrived. Many area grocery stores offer online shopping. You can actually do your grocery shopping in the middle of the night or whenever you can find the time to do it. Merely sitting at your computer, you can choose what you want to buy. You can pay extra to have it delivered to your home or some stores have it set up where you order the food and they pick it out for you and bag it for you, and you come in and pick it up.

Easy Dinner Ideas

Crock Pot

The crock pot was invented for busy people like you! You can make so many different types of things in the crock pot and while you are out having a busy day, your dinner is cooking away at home and will be ready whenever you need it. Most meats can be cooked—be creative, add vegetables and a little water and turn it on low for the whole day. You can also make soups and keep them warm in the crock pot.

Here are a few easy ideas to for your crock pot.

Pork Chops In the Crock Pot
Ingredients:
2-4 thick porkchops
2-4 potatoes, peeled, cut into chunks
2-4 carrots, peeled, cut into chunks
1 onion, peeled, cut into chunks

Set the ingredients in the crock pot and put about an inch of water in it. Salt to taste and cook on low for at least five hours. If you are really in a hurry, you can just throw the porkchops, several potatoes (whole with skins on), some carrots that you bought at the store already peeled and ready to eat, and an onion you peeled and cut in half into the crock pot. You will still get a good meal. The pork chops can be substituted for any meat and the veggies can be broccoli, cauliflower, zucchini or anything you can think of.

Barbecue
There is just something about grilling outside in the summer that just creates a family atmosphere. If you are busy, but you love that taste of barbecue, try cooking a lot at once. Cook chicken and hamburgers at the same time. Have the hamburgers tonight and put the chicken in a pan with barbecue sauce and warm it up tomorrow night. It is a wonderful way to have a "home cooked" meal waiting for them and all you have

Meals are great times to communicate.

to do is warm it up.

Barbecueing is not just for meat. You can barbecue vegetarian meat patties or tofu. Fish-ka-bobs are also a good idea and fun to make. You can put almost any type of fish on your ka-bobs. Some good items to include are fish-ka-bobs, scallops, crabmeat, shrimp, fish fingers or any type of fish, onions, tomatoes, asparagus and zucchini.

Drizzle some butter on the kabobs and set them on the grill. There is another bar-b-q idea listed at the end of this section.

Other Good Time Saving Ideas
Easy Supper Casserole
Make it ahead of time and have it in the dish ready to pop into the oven if you want to to really cut your time.
Ingredients:
5 potatoes (sliced, skins can be left on)
3 onions (peeled and sliced)
1 can of corn (drained)
1 can of tomatoes
8 link pork sausages

In casserole dish: A layer of sliced potatoes, layer of sliced onions, layer of canned tomatoes, layer of canned corn. Repeat the process until casserole dish is filled. Add part of the juice from the tomatoes, for moisture. lay the pork sausages across the top.

Bake 45 minutes or longer until potatoes are tender, turning the sausages occasionally. While it is baking, do something fun with your kids.

Chicken Noodle Soup
Ingredients:

Chicken (can be a whole chicken you dump in the pot, or it can be boneless breast of chicken you either put in whole or cut up; whatever is easiest for you)
Sliced, peeled carrots (two or three carrots)
Peeled and cut up onion (about two)
Sliced celery (about three stalks)
Salt, pepper, or garlic salt to taste

In a large pot or crock pot, place the chicken, carrots, onions and celery. Cook on the stove at least two hours, in crock pot, all day on low, the last half hour on high. If you use boneless chicken, you may want to add some bouillon for more flavoring. About half an hour before you will serve it, add the noodles. This gives you half an hour to do something with your children.

Stir Fry Dinners
Stir fry night is a fun night for everybody. This gets the kids involved with the cooking and you are having fun while you make it.

Tofu Stir Fry
Ingredients:
Tofu
Vegetable oil
Clove of garlic, chopped (or just garlic salt if you don't have time)
1 teaspoon dry mustard
1/8 cup tamari sauce (or to taste)
Shelled Sunflower Seeds
Cut up potatoes, carrots and broccoli

Brown the tofu in the oil (a wok is best, but it can be

made in a frying pan). Add garlic, mustard and a little water as it cooks to avoid sticking. Take turns letting the kids stir (watch out for the hot pan) Add tamari to taste. Cook the potatoes, stirring constantly. Add carrots, broccoli and sunflower seeds. Put a lid on it and cook for about a minute or two – just enough for you to get your children to help you set the table and get the drinks.

Chicken, Beef, Shrimp, or Pork Stir Fry

Stir fry dinners can be made with almost anything. The above recipe would be fine if you substituted any type of meat or some types of fish. You can try experimenting. Butter is a good marinade for scallops or shrimp. Teriyaki sauce is good with beef and chicken. If you look at the grocery stores, there are special stir fry sauces, and they even have vegetables already cut up and ready to drop into your hot oil. This takes away from the fun of chopping up the ingredients with your child, but it helps if you are really in a hurry for a fast, yet healthy meal.

Good Old Meatloaf

Meatloaf is an inexpensive and very easy meal, and it just screams comfort food, good old days, and simpler times. Health conscious cooks might want to consider using ground turkey or any other type of ground meat, but here is a good recipe for basic meatloaf like your grandma used to fix.

Ingredients:

1 1/2 pound lean ground beef or chuck

1/2 cup chopped onion

1 egg, beaten

1/2 cup oatmeal (straight from the box – the "quick oats" version)

1 teaspoon garlic salt
1 teaspoon Worcestershire sauce
salt and pepper
1 cup tomato juice

Here's a fun thing to do with the kids. Make sure they wash their hands. Mix together the ingredients with your hands. If the consistency is not right, add a little of this, a little of that (above measurements are estimates—that's the way grandma made it). Shape the mixture into loaves. Bake at 350° for 45-60 minutes. Pour ketchup on top right before you take it out of the oven. If you make two small loaves, you can freeze one and use it some day when you do not have time to make dinner.

An Easy Sunday Morning Brunch Dish
Ingredients:
1 pkg. (24 oz.) frozen shredded hash browns (thawed)
1/3 cup melted butter
1 cup (4 oz.) shredded cheddar cheese
1 cup shredded swiss (if you just have cheddar, the use 2 cups cheddar)
1 cup diced cooked ham (or bacon or whatever you have)
1 cup milk
4 eggs (mix the eggs with the milk and set aside)
1/2 tablespoon salt and pepper

Grease pie plate, press thawed hash brown into the pie plate, Use a paper towel to remove excess moisture. Brush hash browns with melted butter and bake at 425° for 25 minutes.

Remove crust and fill with layers of ham, cheese and then the eggs and milk. Cook at 350° for 30-40 minutes.

Super Easy Quiche for Dinner or Breakfast
Ingredients:
1 frozen pie crust
6-8 eggs
Cheddar cheese
Whatever else you want to add: chopped onions, chopped peppers, mushrooms

Poke holes in the bottom of the pie crust pan. Mix the eggs with a little milk and pour into the pie crust. Add whatever else you want to. (Note: if your kids hate mushrooms, don't add them...put whatever they like in it) Add most of the cheese, holding a little back to sprinkle on it when it is almost cooked. Cook about an hour, checking occasionally to see how it looks.

Pasta Con Broccoli
Great to make ahead and keep warm in the crock pot.
Ingredients:
1/2 lb. pasta shells (jumbo or larger)
1/2 stick butter or margarine
small bunch broccoli (or just use frozen)
salt, pepper, garlic to taste
2 cups half and half
8 oz. tomato sauce
1/2 lb. fresh mushrooms (optional)
1 cup parmesan cheese
1/2 cup romano cheese

Sauté mushrooms in garlic and butter, add the half and half, tomato sauce and cheese. Next add the cooked pasta and then the cooked broccoli. You could make it the day before and either warm it up or put it in the crock pot. Add a little milk or water so it will not dry out.

Hearty Muffins

Here's a trick your family will enjoy!

Buy the ready-made muffin mixes (which can be very inexpensive). Add fresh fruit to the mixture, and cook according to the directions on the box.

Apple muffins can be made by adding small apple slices to an apple muffin mix. Banana muffins will taste better with fresh bananas in them, also.

Chapter 6
Taking The Hassles Out Of
Homework and Household Chores

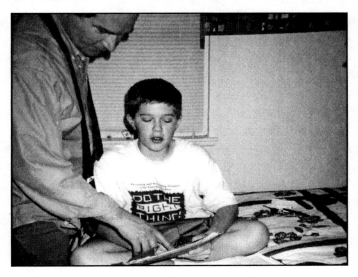

Getting clear agreements about everyday household chores is a must for busy families today. With more and more moms in the work force, it is even more important that the duties at home are divided up among the family members. The days of leaving it all for super mom to handle are a distant memory for most households today. Here are some suggestions about how to create a system of cooperation including parents and kids.

Attitude

If you live by the paradigm that you are responsible for everybody and everything, then you might first like to experience an attitude adjustment and then fire yourself to boot. Drop the martyr thing, know that you deserve to take care of yourself and move on. The cost of hanging onto the old paradigm is increasing resentments, frustration, anger and exhaustion. Then everyone around you suffers. People in that state of mind are miserable to live with. Consider rethinking those beliefs about your need to be in control or responsible for everyone's happiness.

Present Your Case

Once you are ready to let go of some of the responsibilities around the house, it is time to take it up with the rest of your crew. Refer back to the chapter on family meetings, for they are the best forum we know of to create win-win agreements that work. Here is how we would advise you to present your case.

"Guys, I have an issue I need help with. I've been feeling resentful and angry about doing most of the household chores and I know I've been crabbing and nagging at you a lot lately about them. I don't want to be in that space and I do not think you like it any better. Let's talk about how we can divide up the chores so that everyone shares in the responsibilities around here and no one feels overburdened."

At this point, you close your mouth (use tape if need be) and listen, really listen to what your kids have to say. Every suggestion or idea is heard and validated whether or not you use it. Everyone has a say, and the less you, the parent, talks the better. The more input your kids have into the final agreement, the more they own it. The more they own the solution, the more the cooperation ensues. This is when you give your kid their say-so, their power, their sense of control.

The result of this brainstorming, problem solving portion of the family meeting is a clear, win-win agreement that works for everyone. The more time you take up front to handle concerns and objections, the easier it will be down the road. We suggest you never decide things by a vote because someone always leaves with hurt feelings and a bad taste in their mouth. Guess who is the first person who is going to sabotage the agreement? You got it. Think how valuable it will be for your kids to have had regular practice at gaining consensus with probably the toughest group they will ever work with, their siblings and parents. Can you think of any group in the world that you have more history and investment with?

Make Sure Everyone Understands

Be sure everyone, parents included, are crystal clear about the agreement, expectations for each person, etc. This makes it easier to follow through with the agreement later on. This is especially true with teenagers. One mom told us once about being frustrated that her 16 year old daughter was breaking agreements and curfews. One

Helping with chores helps kids feel valuable.

Sunday night at 6:00, she told her daughter she could go study with her friend as long as she came home at 8:00 "and by the way, please clean up your room before you go" she added. At 8:00, no daughter. Still no daughter at 8:10, 8:15, and finally it was 8:20. The daughter waltzes in nonchalantly and her mom was livid.

"You told me you would be home at 8:00!" she said. "I can't believe you are defying me like this!"

"Hold on mom," her daughter said. "You told me I could stay out until 8:00. That was two hours. It took me 20 minutes to clean my room, so I didn't leave until 6:20 so I figured I could stay out until 8:20."

That is teen logic at its best! Here the problem was that neither side took the time to get really clear about their agreements. Don't you make the same mistake.

Try Out The Agreement

At the end of the discussion, decide to try out the new agreement for a few weeks and then check back in at a family meeting to see how it is working. Trust that because you took the time to hear and use everyone's input and concerns and because everyone feels like it was a win-win, they have ownership of the agreement and you will get great cooperation. In our experience, the family responds well and you will have weeks or months of good compliance. If things start to slide, at a family meeting, bring the issue back onto the table and see what's up. Maybe someone is tired of their job and wants to trade off. Maybe it's the end of school and they have spring fever. Whatever, work out the kinks, re-commit everyone to their new agreement and once again you are on your way. Isn't that better than nagging and whining and yelling day in and day out?

Everyone Can Help Out

Even young children can help out. Everyone likes to feel valuable and that they are contributing. Serving others and being valuable are two of the best vehicles for children or adults to feel good about themselves. Start them early. Empower them. Stretch them. Give them training about how to make their bed, do their wash, or cut the grass and then let go and watch them grow. Kids love a challenge. Don't just give them the titles of trashman and busboy. Early teens can help to balance check books; middle schoolers can cut the lawn. Children can plant, weed, and water flower gardens. Be creative. Ask them what they would like to take over and you may be surprised at their responses.

When you have become successful at sharing the household duties, you will experience tremendous benefits. Your kids will feel more empowered, important and valuable. You will feel more rested, relaxed and patient.

You may even free up some time for your efforts. That time can be spent taking better care of yourself and the children. That time can be spent playing with your kids and your spouse. Who couldn't use more of all three? Go for it. You will not regret it and neither will your kids.

Chapter 7
So Many Activities, Sports, and Lessons...So Little Time

It seems like every year our children become busier and busier and this causes the parents to be busier. For every lesson Johnny or Susie is in, a parent must drive the child. For sports teams there are practices, games, meetings and outings. Families have difficulty keeping up with all of the hectic schedules of their children, but when they add their own activities it can seem a bit overwhelming.

Make A Good Calendar

A good calendar can be the key to organizing your family's activities. There are different ways to achieve a good calendar. Some families like to use a large sheet of white paper and post it where everyone can see it every day. You can do this week by week or month by month. Other families use one master datebook. All activities must be on this book. Each member may have their own individual planners, but everything must be put in the "official book." The computer is another alternative to helping organize the family. There are calendar programs which you can use to put your family's activities on. The computer printouts are good because they can be updated and passed out weekly, having one posted on the refrigerator in case people lose their copies.

Children must be given a certain amount of responsibility for the calendars. If they are invited to a party and do not put it on the calendar, they can only hope someone will be available to drive them that day. If everyone goes over their individual schedules it will be better because everyone will be able to see what the others have planned.

Carpool

Carpooling is a good way to reduce the number of car trips per day. If your son is on a baseball team and the neighbor is on the same team, maybe you could take the boys to practice and the neighbor could bring them home. It saves you driving one way.

Schedule Classes Together

One way you can save yourself a trip is to try to get things scheduled at the same time in the same place. For example if your daughter wants to take a dance class at the YMCA, maybe you could schedule your son's swimming lesson at the same place around the same time, so you will only be making one trip. Music lessons can often be lined up back to back. If both kids take piano, ask the teacher if you can schedule one first and while the other is waiting for his or her lesson, you can be working on homework. Anytime you can accomplish two things with the steps of one, you are saving yourself.

Sometimes You Have To Say "No"

Kids often get so excited they want to sign up for everything they find out about. They need time to play, and when they are overscheduled it can be hard to find any down time. Some parents choose to say their children can only play one sport during a season. This might be the best option especially if the child is in scouts or taking a musical instrument lesson.

Use Your Time In The Car Together Wisely

As long as you are going to have to drive your children to their lessons, sports, or activities, you may as well use the time in the car to your advantage. There are several ways to do this. If the child has a test coming up, you could go over it together. The car is also a good time to get your child to talk. Ask him or her about their day, what they are doing in their lives, what their hopes and dreams are.

You can even use this time to talk to them about drugs, sex, or anything that may be difficult to start a conversation with face to face. Casually bring it up and see where it leads to.

Some people find it easier to talk to their children when they are in the car, with the radio casually playing in the background, or the windows open and the sounds of the outside all around them. Still others find the ride in the car is a good time to have a prayer together. There are so many wonderful things that can come out of conversation with your children in the cars if we only take the opportunity to use that time wisely.

Chapter 8
Sometimes You Get Sick

Let's talk a moment about illnesses and their repercussions. Illness encompasses several different aspects. There are those days when a mom with small children is sick and she must figure out how to be the best mom she can be while confined to a bed. (A single dad or a dad whose wife is out of town faces the same problem). Another topic of illness is when the child is sick and still another is when the parent has become very ill and the lifestyle may have to change because of it. Whether it is you who is sick, or your child, it may take a little planning to keep the kids feeling grounded at a time when there is such upheaval.

You Don't Feel Well, But The Kids Are Home

Most of the time a parent can pop a pain reliever and get on with the daily routine. As a parent, we rarely have time to get sick. Sometimes it happens that nothing you take will help, such as the pain experienced from a migraine or an upset stomach. Morning sickness is another example. These ills can confine you to a bed and there is nothing you may be able to do about it for a while.

If your child is an infant, it will not be too difficult because you can lay down next to where the baby is sleeping and it will not be too hard for you to take care of the baby. You can wheel the bassinets into your bedroom if it is convenient. There may be outbursts of crying from the child, but if he or she is in bed or a crib, there is nothing life-threatening going on with the child.

If your child is a toddler, that is an entirely different story. One thing that works is to lay the child down with you and turn on the television to shows he might enjoy watching. If you have someone who can come and get the child, it might help you out and also might avoid the child from getting sick. If you do not have help, you can get through this by yourself. You will have to be a little less structured. If you do not allow your child to watch more than a certain amount of television, you might want to relax that rule. You need the rest and if the TV is keeping your child occupied, at least he is out of harm's way.

Besides television, you can get your child to do an activity. If you have a craft box, maybe this is a good time to bring it out. Have her sit quietly and work on a craft. Do not worry too much if she leaves a mess, maybe dad can clean it up when he gets home or you can get it later when you are feeling better.

With older kids, you can occupy their time by getting

them to do things for you. Most kids will want to help a parent who is sick, so if you say "could you get me a drink?" or "could you set the table" or even "could you fix dinner?" they will generally be happy to be able to help and you will be able to know what they are doing by instructing them. They will also feel a certain amount of pride later when you brag on them for the great job they did of taking care of you.

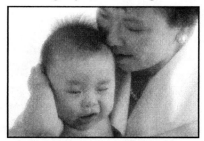
Sick kids need special attention.

If you feel you really need to sleep, make sure the children are taken care of first. If they are old enough, and the doors are locked, you could set a timer and take a nap. Let the child see you set the timer. Tell her what you expect of her while you are sleeping. "I am setting this timer for 30 minutes so I can take a nap and maybe get rid of this headache, you can watch this show during that time. Please do not go anywhere, just watch the show and then when it is over, could you please come and check with me to be sure I woke up." This will do two things, it will let them know you intend to take a nap, but you know what they are supposed to be doing, and it will also get them to check in with you in half an hour.

Parent Is Injured

When a parent is injured, for instance breaks an arm or leg, there are certain changes that need to take place in the home.

When I broke my elbow, there were just certain things I could not do. I could not carry the laundry basket or

anything that required both hands. Anything that need-
ed to be unscrewed, like my pain medication or the salsa
jar, was also impossible. My husband tried to help out
as much as possible, getting up early to clean up the
house and make the breakfasts for everyone, and also
doing the laundry. He has always s been active in help-
ing with the household chores, but he went overboard
trying to do it all to make things easier on me. When he
did all of the work, the boys did not need to, and I began
to think that maybe they should be included. I discov-
ered that by asking the boys to do some of these chores,
it both gave them a sense of inclusion and value in help-
ing out the family, and it took some of the edge off of my
husband.

S.T.R.

Your Child Is Sick

You have to work, your spouse has to work, and suddenly, in the midst of running around getting everyone
ready for work and school, you hear it. "Mommy, I don't
feel very good," or "Daddy, I'm sick." One of you will have
to stay home from work unless you have made other
arrangements for days when your children are sick. It is not
our intent to help you decide which of you will have to take
off work, it is merely our intent to help you know some
things you can do with your child while he or she is home
sick from school.

Everyone has to make their own tough decisions about
their children. Secretaries have had children sleeping under
their desk because they absolutely had to be at work that
day. Do what you think is necessary, but keep the child's
best interest first.

As children get older, they tend to appear that they do

not need their parents as much as they did when they were younger. They run around happily exploring everything the world has to offer. When they are sick, they want their parents. If you just leave your child alone when he is sick or if you turn on the television and go off in another room for the entire day, you will miss a very special and tender time.

Children will remember the nurturing and the tender loving care their parents give them when they are sick. That is why the *Chicken Soup* books have become so popular. Chicken soup brings connotations of that soup your mom made you when you were not feeling well as a child. She made you feel better just by being there. Keep a can of chicken soup in the cupboard for such an occasion. You probably have other memories of when you were younger and were not feeling well. Maybe it is grape juice or a special bell you could ring when you wanted your parents, or a special "friend" stuffed animal who slept with you when you were sick. Take the time to take care of your children when they are sick.

If your son is lying there feeling a bit punk, maybe now is a good time to bring out that A.A. Milne book and read to him the stories of Winnie the Pooh. Even if he seems too old to be read to, if your child is sick, he will appreciate it. Often we are so busy we do not find enough time (although we should make the time) to read to our children. A day in bed is a perfect day to make up for that lost time.

Another fun thing to do is turn on tapes, CDs, or old records that the child can listen to. They need their rest, but they can get bored just laying there, so listening to the music, reading, or doing a craft is a good way to occupy them.

If your child feels really sick and just does not want to sit up and do a craft or watch television or anything; he probably just wants to sleep. Check in on him every once in a while so he will not feel so alone.

If you are in the other room and hear your child throwing up, immediately go to be with him or her. There is nothing more lonely than being by yourself when you are getting sick. Gently placing your hand on the child's stomach will help give them support and avoid that cramping feeling. It will also reinforce to your child that you are right there.

A Child Is Seriously Ill

Routine illness is one thing, but every parent's nightmare is having a child become seriously ill or injured. There are several things you will need to remember to take care of. First of all, the sick child is the main focus. Try to make sure he or she is able to ask any questions and that you are open to talk about the illness. There is no reason to scare the child, but it is good to let them talk about it. Often, you do not have to answer the tough questions, you can just respond with a question of our own.

If she asks you "what will happen to me?" You can respond with, "What do you think will happen?" or something that will let her know you are there for her. Often, a child will veer off the subject once you start asking questions back.

Another thing you need to remember is if there are other children in the family, their lives will be disrupted and they might be feeling scared. Be sure to keep the lines of communication open to them as well, and depending on their age, only offer the information they need to know. There is no reason to make a child any more fearful than they already are. If the sick child is receiving lots of presents or balloons, maybe get something for the other children and encourage sharing. They will want to know their sibling is ok, so if possible let them visit or call on the telephone if the child is in the hospital.

My sister and brother-in-law were just incredible when their youngest daughter was in the hospital. They would take turns staying at the hospital and the other parent would be at home to be with the other children. It was important to my sister that one of them were there to greet the kids every day when they got home from school. She would be at the hospital all day, and then have someone come to the hospital to sit with my niece and she would go home to be with the other two.

They did not do a lot of whispering around the children. They were open and let the kids ask questions and they answered them to the best of their ability. The daily routine of life in the family was kept as normal as possible. The girls made it to their basketball and volleyball games because other family members pitched in and helped out. This was where having a great family came in handy. Everyone stuck together and helped each other. It was a good example for the girls and for their cousins, my sons, as to how important your family really is.

One day, one of the children called their dad from school because she was scared. She called him at work and said, "I can't stop thinking about her, can you come and pick me up?" My brother-in-law said, "Well, I could come, but then there would just be two sad people together. If we both stay where we are, we will be with other happy people and we can try to make it until after school." She agreed and they both made it through the day. It was that listening to her that helped her. She knew he was there for her.

S.T.R.

Chapter 9

Kids Out Of School? Don't Panic!

Different parts of the country have their school breaks at different times of the year. Many areas have year 'round school and if you are involved in this type of educational system, you have the challenge of coming up with activities at different times of the year. Other areas still have the summer break system. Whatever your situation is, you have the same problem, or blessing (depends on how you look at it): your kids are home and you need to find ways to keep them happy and occupied.

Kids get increasingly excited about vacation from school. It is extra time to play outside and they might even get to sleep late. As a mom or dad managing that change in your schedule, just thinking about those long days can make you want to pull your hair out. What do you do to make the vacation time the best ever for you and your children? There are many helpful things you can do. One of the most important, however, is to develop the right attitude. Having your kids around is a *good* thing! They are only young for so long, and then they will not want to be around. Take advantage of the closeness you can develop while they are young.

Start Early

The most important thing you can do to make the off-time successful is to start before school is even out and have a family meeting to discuss plans and the changes that will be occurring. Make agreements about wake-up time, bedtime, TV and even electronic game limits. It is best to reach family consensus about these things vs. when mom and dad just set the rules like a dictatorship. It is more fun and things seem to run much smoother when everyone has input and is in agreement.

Specialized Day Camps

Check out those vacation specials for day camps. There are many different types such as art, music, drama, computer camps. Look in your local newspapers, parenting publications, local YMCA, etc. Try to find the things your children are really interested in. Go for the things they love to do, not necessarily what you want them to excel at or think they should do. Make sure you save time in their schedules for just hanging out around the house or playing with friends.

Volunteer Possibilities

If you have young teens, check out the volunteer possibilities early in the year, such as helping out an animal shelter if the child has an interest in animals; or volunteering at a daycare program if they show a love and interest in children. Organizations of all kinds are always eager to find

help from young people that have an interest in what they do.

Some parents allow their pre-teens or teenagers to make up flyers about their expertise such as lawn service or baby sitting. We

There are many different kinds of special camps in the summer.

have even heard of some young teens who created little day camps in their backyard for neighborhood kids complete with puppets, games, snacks, water play, etc.

Let's Have A Show!

Another thing that is fun is to have a neighborhood production. One energetic teen got her neighborhood friends to put on *The Wizard of Oz*. They had practices all summer and a production date. On that day, they had programs printed and charged an admission. This provided a world of opportunities for kids who enjoyed acting, working on the costumes, the sets, and the programs. They divided up the profits amongst themselves. There was not much money to be made, but they sure had a good time working on it.

Ask Around

For your peace of mind, ask around for recommendations on high school or college kids that might want a standing job baby-sitting for you each week. Even if it is only for a few hours, for a stay at home mom or dad, that time you can have alone is important for you to have and call your own. Use that time to schedule your appointments, grocery shop in peace or just take a walk in your favorite place alone.

Do Not Overschedule Your Children

In this hectic, rushed pace we find ourselves in, vacation time should be a time to unwind and relax a little, along with discovering the joys a holiday from school can bring. Encourage outings in your own backyard or your neighborhood pool. Rushing kids from camp to camp, lessons to lessons, etc. may not be fun for your child all summer. Kids today need time to just be and discover their world and have time to themselves.

Plan Trips to Local Places

Take your kids to the places they might go to on a field trip at school. How about the zoo, local museums, or an animal farm. Do something special like this each week so everyone can look forward to a new adventure and rediscover their own community.

Do Not Forget About Relatives

Out of town or even in town, they may enjoy helping out now and then and keep your kids overnight or even for a short "vacation." Visiting a grandparent or favorite aunt can be a wonderful memory for children as well as give mom and dad a break. Encourage support of your significant other in helping out with their favorite summertime activities. For example, if your husband likes to roller blade and you like to bike, switch off taking the kids to do these things with you. Better yet, find something everyone can do, like go to a baseball game or other sporting event.

Remember what you enjoyed doing as a kid in the summertime or when you were on vacation and let your kids find their favorite things. If you enjoyed having lemonade stands, try letting your children have one and see how they like it.

I remember being quite the entrepreneur, always trying to "sell" people at my lemonade stands or with my homemade bakery goods. My children also enjoy selling real snow-cones and have learned a lot of neat things standing on the street corner in our neighborhood. They have some great stories to tell after a "day at work" selling snow-cones. Sometimes the simplest things make the fondest memories.

A.J.

We started a neighbor-hood newspaper one summer, and it really kept us occupied going up to the neighbors and asking if they had any "news" to contribute to the paper. We also got to know the neighbors bet-ter. Maybe it even helped

Having a refreshment stand can be a lot of fun on a summer day.

me in the early days of my writing career! Another thing we did was have "Miss America Pageants" where the "contestants," who were all of the girls I played with, would practice their talents and drag out all sorts of cos-tumes and jewelry for the show. Still another memory I have of things we did when we were little was go-cart races. We would get our dads to find us some old wheels and wood to make go-carts , then we would set a time for the "big race." We would start at the top of our street where someone would push you and you'd go flying. We had a lot of fun with simple things.

S.T.R.

Make Sure You Make Time For The Children

The vacations from school can sometimes add more to a parent's schedule than he or she thinks she can handle. Try to remember that your children are important and if it means making that phone call a little later, let your child know he or she is important. There is a television commercial where a busy mom is getting ready for work and her little daughter says, "Mommy, when can I be a client?" It's important to keep them first.

Chapter 10
Making A Move...
Across Town or Across the Country

Moving can be a very stressful time for grownups and that stress is often transferred to the children. They feel tension in the air and have apprehensions about what is going on. Many times they will react to the stress around them in ways that confuse parents (more misbehavior, outbursts, withdrawal).

It is important to take the time to talk to your children about moving no matter what age they are. If you are moving far away, show them on a map. Explain how easy it will be to stay in touch with friends and travel back and forth. Even if you do not plan to travel back and forth or if it is very far, show them that it is possible to reconnect to friends with air travel, driving, the train, or bus. The more chances kids have to express their thoughts and feelings about the move, the more easily it will be for them to let go and move on. Let them know it may be a little hard for everyone to make the adjustments but you will all work together and the result will be a better life where you are going. Let your children know what to expect so there will be no surprises. There are so many ways you can help children adjust to their new home.

Keep In Touch With Friends

One thing that helps ease the sadness of leaving friends and family behind is the promise to keep in touch. If finances will allow it, let your children use the telephone and call their friends long distance. The separation difficulties usually go away in a week or so because most children make friends fairly quickly. Grown-ups take a little longer, so allow yourself some time to call back and forth to your old friends. We all love friends in our lives to help us feel grounded. They will appreciate the call too because they will also miss you.

Let us say your son has a best friend, Chris, when he left behind. Once you get to your new house and the parents are busy with the moving activities there will probably come a time where your son will be missing Chris. Kids can feel lonely and a bit scared when they are in a new place. If the parents take the time to notice when the child is feeling lonely, the child will feel better and not so alone. If you see he is looking lonesome, tell him "you can call Chris tonight." The reason for postponing the call (besides the fact that the rates are usually cheaper at night) is it will give your son something to look forward to. After a while of being in the new place, your son will find things to occupy his time, and he will want to call Chris less and less. Chris will understand because he will be taking new steps to find a new friend also. If you do not make an effort to help your children maintain contact with their old friends during the transition, they could feel their friendships are not worth much. Teach your children the value of a friend and encourage your children to write letters to their friends or communicate on the Internet (with your supervision).

Make The New Place Look Like Home

As soon as you get the furniture unloaded off the truck and in the children's room, open the box of their "things." If they see their pictures, their trophies, their stuffed animals, whatever is special to them, they will feel more at home. Make sure you get their curtains up soon so they will not be afraid.

Try to give kids as much say so as possible about which room is theirs, where they want their bed situated, where they want their posters and pictures. Kids can lose a sense of control over their life during a move because they usually do not have a choice in the matter. Look for ways for them to be in control and have a say-so and choices. This will help them settle in easier.

After you get the children's room set up, try to set up a family area, whether it is the kitchen table area or the living room area. In the midst of all the boxes and blank walls there should be small havens where you can go and feel comfortable. It is an adjustment for you too, and you need a place to feel homey and to be able to relax.

Though you are busy putting things where they belong and moving things, make time to sit together those first days you are in your new house. Order a pizza if you have to and sit in the area you have cleaned out. If you have not cleared an area out yet, sit on boxes. Talk about everyone's concerns and plans for tomorrow. Try to get the children enthusiastic about their new home and help them look forward to something you will be doing the next day.

Get Involved In Activities

A Cub Scout in Washington, D.C. looks just like a Cub Scout in Phoenix, Ariz. A Girl Scout in Dallas, Texas looks just like a Girl Scout in Carmel, Ind. The same can be said about baseball players, soccer players, and tae kwon do enthusiasts. If your child was involved in an activity back home, try to find that same activity in your next town. Team sports and scouts are excellent ways for both children and their parents to meet people and find a place to fit in.

Sports and clubs can help boost a child's confidence, while providing a quick and easy way to make friends. If the parent offers to help coach, they will be able to forge into this new world of making friends in a strange town together. The other parent can come to the games and meet the other parents on the team.

The New Kid

Whenever you move to a new place, your child automatically becomes the "new kid." That can be a very special thing. Rather than allowing your child to feel left out or unpopular, turn it around and point out the great things about being the new kid. These advantages go for the parents, too. Everybody wants to meet you if you are new. They want to hear about where you have come from; it is a good conversation piece.

Take a walk around the streets near your house and be on the lookout for toys that match your children's age. Evening walks in the spring and summer usually allow you to meet lots of kids and parents out in their yards. Drop your shyness and meet people. Your kids will be playing with the neighbors' kids before your chit-chat is over. Get phone numbers, plan a barbecue and you are on your way. Don't wait for your neighbors to come over with a plate of cookies; take some over to them if you have to.

People want to get you to join their organizations. For the kids, they want them to join the teams and scouts mentioned previously. For the parents, they want you to join their parent organization at the school; they want you to be a coach or a leader; they want to get you on a committee. This is a perfect time to consider your options while meeting people. Let people talk to you under the guise of trying to get you to do something. You can listen to them and get to know them. It helps in trying to figure out where everyone fits in your new surroundings. It is a perfectly understandable excuse to say, "thanks for asking me, but since we just moved here, I want to get more adjusted before I take on anything."

The alternative would be to say, "Sure I'd love to." The more things you can get yourself into the better. Children will adjust quicker to their new surroundings. It does take some effort on a grown-up's part, especially the parent who did not move there for his or her job. If it is your husband whose job caused the move, you may have more trouble adjusting. He will meet friends at work and that will occupy his time. If you join a committee, get a job, or volunteer somewhere, you will soon begin meeting people and you will have something to look forward to yourself.

Dr. Laura Schlessinger, the psychologist, likes to use the motto "I'm my kid's mom" (or I'm my kid's dad), which stresses the importance of putting our kids first. Even she has a job. In our efforts to keep our kids grounded and be the best parent we can be, there has to be a time where we do other things. You do not have to have a job, but you could have a hobby, be on a committee, be a group leader or volunteer in your child's class. By broadening your own horizons you will be helping your children by being a happier person and you will be strengthening your marriage by being more well-rounded and content and bringing more to the marriage.

Volunteer In Your Child's Class

This can be one of the most useful ways of helping your child feel comfortable in their new school. Go up to the school and meet the teacher and walk around with the child. Get to feel comfortable there along with your child. Talk one on one with your child's teacher and try to set up a time you can come in to volunteer if it is at all possible. If you work all day and cannot possibly do it, maybe you could send treats for a special day. (Everybody sends treats on Halloween, Christmas and Valentine's Day)

If you do work and find it impossible to volunteer, maybe you could just take off work for a few hours to come over and share with the class something interesting; for instance, if you came from Washington, D.C. you could bring some things about that. Anything you can do to get to know your child's classmates would help your child feel grounded and help you get a feel for their new environment and friends.

Some parents try to arrange their schedules so they can help out in the class or be available. School usually starts early. If you can come in to work at say 10:00 once a week, maybe you can help with the children's writing. The teachers are usually so happy to get parent volunteers they will bend over backwards to work around your schedule. A teacher who knows the parents are going to treat that student differently than one who has never met them. If your child is having trouble adjusting and you talk to the teacher about it, chances are the teacher will take the extra time to help the student. If the teacher does not know there is a problem, he or she will not be able to work with your child.

Another way you can make your children know you are there for them is to be there when they get home from school. There are so many parents who just cannot do that because they have to work, so their children go to day care, after school programs or go home to an empty house. If you can arrange your schedule to where you get off at 3:00 and your children get home at 3:20, you will be there to hear how their day went. When you first move to a new town it is especially comforting for a child to see his or her parents. They have been around strangers all day long and it is nice to see a friendly face.

Take Advantage Of The Fact Your Children Do Not Know Anyone

This may sound strange, but the fact that your children do not know many people may actually be beneficial to the family unit at first. In your other home you were creatures of habit with everyone having their own places to go and things to do. Now that you are new, it is a good chance to explore everything together. Go to the museums as a family. Take picnics and go on family camp-outs. Soon your kids will have friends and will want to do sleepovers at their houses or will be busy with activities. You have a great opportunity to plan some really great camp-outs or short weekend trips together.

Make Yourself Over

If you have never been a camping family, maybe your move is a good time to start. You can be or do anything you want to in your new place because people have no pre-dispositions about you. If the children have never taken horseback riding lessons and you move to the west, with stables nearby, go sign them up. Perhaps you have always wanted to dress a little more casual, to get away from that uptight stereotype you had; do it. Maybe you like hats but were afraid to wear them. The kids like cowboy boots but you never wore them where you came from. Anything is possible when you just move to a new place.

Signing up for a baseball team or joining an organization is another way to help a "new kid" fit in.

Sometimes kids want to make themselves over, also. A new haircut is a good start. Maybe your son has been wanting a "buzz" cut, but you were adamantly against it. What was your reasoning? Is there a legitimate reason? If there really is not one, why not let him try it (hair grows back). And what about that daughter of yours who has been begging to get her ears pierced or has been wanting to take piano lessons. With a new surrounding comes a new enthusiasm and you could feed on it while you can.

Try To Find A Surrogate Family

If you are far away from your extended family as a result of the move, you may experience several problems. Holidays can be lonely, the kids miss the spontaneity of going over to visit family, but one of the biggest ones is no baby-sitter. If you can find a family who is similar to you then maybe you can exchange baby-sitting, have them over to cook-outs on holidays and go to their houses for dinners. Depending on where you move it can be easy or hard to find such a family. If someone back home knows a friend and tells you to call them, you should take them up on it. You might get invited over for dinner and it might turn out you like the people. They will know you are not from there and need help every once in a while. Another thing they can do for you is help you with directions , suggestions for doctors, and other questions you may have.

In a big city where you do not know anyone it may be tougher to find a family to be friends with but it is worth the effort. Try to notice on the holidays who stays in town. Ask people you meet how long they have lived there. So many people move these days that there are displaced people all over the place who would probably love to meet another nomad.

Chapter 11
So You're Starting A New Job

It can be an exciting time when a parent changes jobs, but it can also be a very stressful time in the family. If you or your spouse unexpectedly loses your job, try to keep it all in perspective. With the economy as it is in this world, people lose their jobs every day and many times it is through no fault of their own. Companies downsize or they go out of business. Losing a job does not have the same negative connotation as it did many years ago. Most people realize that but for a break here or there, it could be them losing their job. The people who do not understand it are the little people: the children.

If the husband loses his job, he will probably be down.

The rest of the family can be an unbelievable support for him (or her) at this time. Knowing he is loved unconditionally by his family can ease the stress and fear. Everyone will be experiencing a variety of feelings at a time like this. Fear is a big one for many parents. Remember that kids are experts at knowing what we are feeling. It is ok and healthy to talk about your fears or your sadness. Your honesty may give kids permission to talk about what THEY are feeling.

As the person who lost the job, you are upset and trying to figure out what you will do next. There are some hidden blessings in losing our job. One major league baseball player was cut from the team the same week his wife was having a baby. He would never have been able to be with his wife for that special time if he had had that job. If you look for the blessings you may find them in your own life. That time you are home looking in the want-ads, can be spent in a self-absorbed funk or as an opportunity. Go out and play catch with your son for a few minutes. It might even pick your spirits up. It's a beautiful day and you have a healthy, happy son. So you lost your job, you'll find another one soon and then you'll be back at work. Enjoy every day to its fullest and teach your kids to do the same.

Remember that we are mirrors and models for our kids. The way you handle problems is the main way your children will learn how to handle them. They might someday be cut from the team, or later in life, lose a job. Do you want to set the example of being devastated and falling apart or would you like to be an example of don't give up, never ever give up.

While you are out of a job, the money situation may be tight. Try to do things as a family even though things are tense. There are things that are free, like parks, visits to friends' houses, some museums, etc. Fishing is relatively free and it is a fun way to get away from the stresses of finding a job.

There will be a lot of time that the unemployed person will need to work on resumes and be making calls. It should be up to the other spouse to help out by taking the kids out and doing things with them. Mommy needs to "work" today, even if "working" is looking in the classified ads, making contacts and generally getting things going. So take your kids on a hike at a nearby park. Go for a drive. Go swimming. When you get home you will have some exciting news to talk about to the one looking for the job. This may even pick up her spirits to hear the fun you all have been having.

After a long day of pounding the pavement and working on finding a job, it is important for that parent to put that out of his mind and have some family time. If you had a job, you should be leaving it at work and concentrating on your family at night, so try doing it now. Get out a board game and play it as a family. Hold a family meeting to decide where you will go on your vacation (even if it may not be until next year, it's fun to think about). Do things together. This is the time you need each other most of all.

Stay on Track

When a person loses a job, it can become very easy to slip into a series of bad habits. Since you do not have to be at work at a certain time you might be tempted to sleep late. After you get up you may decide there is no rush in getting dressed or maybe you do not even feel like getting dressed for the day. Try not to change very many of your habits. This is a time you need to eat healthy meals, exercise and get plenty of rest—but not too much. If you work at it, you will be able to keep your gumption and it will not be so difficult to begin looking for a new job.

Chapter 12
Are We There Yet?
Traveling With Youngsters

"Are we there yet?" "How much farther?" "I gotta go!" These are all too familiar when you are in the car taking a family trip. The whole idea seems so fun when you plan it, but when the big day comes you are all stressed out from packing and making deadlines just to get ready for the trip. When you cram everything and everyone into the car, it can all seem to go down the tubes. There are ways you can plan ahead in order to have a great trip right from the start.

Different aged kids enjoy different things, but the little ones enjoy getting "presents," so a fun thing to do is wrap about 10 different things up and set times when you will let the child open them. Say every three hours you will get a present. These presents can be a box of crayons, a can of play-doh, a pack of cards, a granola bar, just little things to keep them occupied. The whole ordeal of waiting for the next prize and then opening it up is fun for the child. They will probably then play for a while with that item or eat that snack, then the anticipation starts up for the next one. This really helps on a long trip, but it does take a bit of preparation to get it ready a few days ahead of time.

Another thing that is fun is to buy them a scrapbook and have them keep a journal with it. You can collect brochures, post cards, even the soaps from the hotel or the sugars from the restaurants. Kids love to tape and glue things into the scrapbook. If you get them some markers, they can then add their own artwork.

Older kids may not be interested in doing crafts or playing cards with their brothers or sisters, but they get just as anxious and bored as little kids. Bring things for them such as an electronic game or some other age appropriate thing. It is good to even have a few surprises for them, such as a new tape of a favorite group you could pop into the tape players, or maybe you could get them their own tape player with headphones so they could listen to their own music.

Books on tape are another fun thing to do providing the whole family is interested in the book. A grown-up or older child can also read a book to the family. It is fun to read about places you are going. Maybe you are driving out west. You could read a book about the Lewis and Clark Trail and talk about the things you are seeing along the way. Whether the trip is for pleasure or you are just driving to get someplace you need to go, you can make the trip fun if you try.

Start Before You Leave

This may sound strange but it is good advice. Decide to start the vacation even before you leave. Shopping for snacks and books and car games can be very fun. Do not be in such a big rush to "get there" that you do not enjoy the trip. Pack footballs and a baseball glove or whiffle ball bat and ball or jump ropes last; and stop at rest areas to play. Those 15-20 minute breaks every three hours allow everyone to stretch and laugh and play. It also stops any of those tense rushed feelings that kids hate to experience with their parents. Who wants to travel with uptight, crabby people? The vacation does not have to begin when you get to the beach. Vacations are really about having fun, close times with your loved ones. You can create that at a highway rest area as well as the beach.

Some Games For The Road Trip

Riddlee-Ree (Also called I See See or I Spy)

This is fun for younger children, but while you are driving down the highway, this game needs to be played using only things inside the car. What you do is pick an object, let's say the driver's red shirt. The person who is "it" says:

"Riddlee-Ree, Riddle-Ree, I see something you don't see and it's red." Everyone takes turns guessing what it is.

The Question Game

This is the advanced version of Riddlee-Ree. The person who is "it" picks a subject. It is more fun if it is a person, but it can be an object. The subject can be in sight or just known to the people playing the game. Everyone takes turns asking "yes" or "no" questions to get the answer. This game is also called Twenty Questions, but in the car with kids, you do not need to limit it to 20 questions. If it starts getting boring, the parent should take over and say, "OK, who is it?" so you can keep the game moving.

Rich Man-Poor Man

This is a fun game especially for children under 12. Bring a catalog along. Choose one person to be "rich man" and one person to be "poor man." "Rich man" gets the most expensive thing on the page and "poor man" gets the most inexpensive. The children will get a real kick out of turning the pages and seeing what each of them get. Take turns being "rich man" or "poor man."

Alphabet List Game

This is an old game, but still it keeps children of all ages occupied. The leader says "I'm going on a trip to (wherever you are going) and I'm going to take an apple." Then the next person says the same thing but adds a Banana or something else that starts with a "B." The next person repeats the previous things and adds a "C" word. You play until someone gets so mixed up they cannot remember them all or until the end of the alphabet.

Alphabet Song Game

This can be played at any time, but it is especially fun if you select categories, such as Holiday Songs or Patriotic Songs etc. One person starts and sings a song that starts with an "A." An example would be "Anchors Aweigh." The second person sings "Boogie Woogie Bugle Boy" or whatever. In order for the game to be fun, you really have to be open-minded and let almost anything count.

Counting Game

This will keep them occupied for a while. Decide what to count. Semi trucks are a good thing. Another thing to count is barns. Say one child gets the barns on the right side of the highway and the other gets the barns on the left side of the highway.

Bingo

It is easy for you to make up your own bingo game. Draw squares and list things you know you will see such as speed limit signs, red barns, cows, green cars, etc. Have the kids just check them off with a pencil and the first one to have all of them filled in is the winner.

The Alphabet City Game

Any game with the alphabet in it is going to last for a while. This one is fun and can be educational. The first person names a city: Boise. The second person has to name a city that begins with the last letter of the word the person before her said: Edmonton. The third person must then name a city which starts with the last letter: New York. For families with varying ages of children, it is good to help the younger ones come up with cities to let them stay in the game longer.

Chapter 13
Living Through Divorce or Other Marital Problems

When parents are having problems in their relationship, it will undoubtedly cause a problem within the family unit as a whole. Parents may think their children do not understand what is going on, and maybe they do not, but they can sense there is something wrong and sometimes not knowing what it is can be just as bad as knowing.

Once you take on the responsibility of having a child, you have certain things you owe them. Security is one of the basic things. If a child goes to bed hearing mommy and daddy yelling and screaming at each other, she might lay there in bed scared about what could come next. Kids watch the news more than we wish they would and they know what goes on. Sometimes marital problems are unavoidable, but there are ways you can keep your kids grounded when it seems like the world around them is coming apart.

Some Ways To Help Keep Your Kids Grounded With Parental Separation

- **Be straight with your child.**
  Give them the facts about the divorce or separation, but only at a level that is appropriate for their understanding. Never blame or badmouth your ex-spouse.

- **Think of your child's feelings and respect them.**
  Let children express their feelings and listen when they talk, but try not to pry.

- **Keep them grounded with their structure and regular daily routine.**
  Try to continue with established rules.

- **Remember your child needs both parents.**
  Encourage your child to have a good relationship with the other parent, also.

- **Remain steadfast as a parent.**
  Remember to be your child's parent and not his friend. Do not make your child have to be your confidant. He or she needs a responsible parent at this time.

- **Never put your child in the situation of being the messenger.**
  Talk to your spouse yourself if there are things you need to discuss with each other. Kids hate being put in the middle of their parent's mischief.

- **Let your child remember the good times.**
Remember together the happy family times before the divorce.

- **Let your child know their life is not over, it will just be different.**
Talk about how through a positive attitude and faith, you can work on your lives and make plans for the future.

- **Read children's books about divorce or separation.**
These may be the starting point for productive talks together.

Chapter 14
You Got A Cash Flow Problem?

Money problems can happen to anyone and when they least expect it. In this economy there are relatively few jobs or professions which are totally stable. There have been very successful white collar workers who, because of the economy have been forced out of work due to their company being shut down. Suddenly finding yourself or your spouse out of work can be devastating for you and it is also very strange for the children. They are used to a certain routine where the parent goes to work every day. Suddenly the parent is home, but not happy and wanting to spend time with them. That same parent is also seen frowning and looking in the newspaper through the want-ads all the time.

Money aside, losing a job is a stressful thing in many ways. Let us use the example in a two parent home of the father who loses his job. His first reaction is either anger, sadness or surprise depending on the circumstances. A supportive wife often feels the same emotions at this point. If it is hard to find employment, the emotions of both change. The father may be feeling inadequate (I should be supporting my family), and the mother may be trying to find ways to keep his spirits up. If his spirits go down, it is harder to look for a job. By constantly trying to help cheer the husband up, the wife may be overlooking her own feelings and needs and a little anger may be setting in. This is causing a tremendous amount of stress in the house which may or may not be coming out in the form of bad tempers, depressed personalities, withdrawn parents. If the parents try to hide it, the children still feel the emotions around them. It is best to talk to the kids and explain what is going on. Daddy lost his job—through no fault of his—we have to work together to help him find one. He will be home but he will be needing to work on his resumes and making contacts so we need to give him the time needed to do that. The father in turn needs to have respect for his wife who is trying to help and he needs to try very hard, even though he is occupied with his own dilemma, to spend some quality time with the rest of the family.

Major league baseball player Rex Hudler was cut by the San Francisco Giants during spring training, shortly before their first daughter was born. Despite being disappointed and concerned for the future, he was able to be with his wife, Jennifer, when she had the baby and was able to enjoy the first few days of his daughter's life. If he was still working then, he would not have had the time off and would have had to leave town shortly after the baby was born. As luck would have it, he was picked up by the California Angels. If he had wasted the time right after he was released to feel depressed and wallow inside himself, he would have missed the beautiful quality time he got to spend with his family. As difficult as it is for us to conceive of any goodness coming out of losing a job, there may be small miracles to be thankful for if we look for them.

When your spouse loses his or her job, there are many emotional things going on, but the plain truth of the matter is you may have to figure out how you are going to pay your bills.

Dealing With Bills

For the first few weeks with no paycheck, people manage to get by either with savings or by just putting off the bills; but there comes a time when bills have to be paid. The first thing you can do to stall the bill collectors is write letters to the companies and explain what happened. Start the letter something like this: "Through no fault of his, my husband has lost his job, and we are having trouble paying our bills. Please accept this partial payment as an honest attempt to pay our bill. Thank you very much." Include whatever you can pay, even if it is only $10. That way, they will have to take a few extra days to write you back and tell you what to do.

If it goes on very long and you get into big trouble with your bills and credit cards, you can contact CCCS (Consumer Credit Counseling Service). They will contact all of the companies you owe money to so they will not keep calling you. It is depressing when you are doing the best you can to get back on your feet and bill collectors keep hounding you. CCCS will help you figure out what you can pay and they can lower your monthly payments. Get the facts on CCCS before you do it because while it is an excellent company that can work for you, it could affect your credit and if you are going to get your job back soon, it may not be worth it to you.

Chapter 15
Staying Connected
With Your Teenager

Teenagers are getting a bad rap today (no pun intended). According to a 1997 survey called "Kids These Days" conducted by Public Agenda, 65% of Americans who have contact with teens describe them disapprovingly. They see teenagers as undisciplined, disrespectful, rude and unfriendly. Many adults are actually afraid of teenagers, lumping them together as all being violent, angry and uncaring. It is no wonder that teens today feel more disconnected from their parents and other adults than perhaps ever before.

A middle-upper class community in St. Louis, Missouri, recently evaluated themselves on whether or not they were providing their youth and teens in particular with the assets

needed for their healthy development. The results were dis-
couraging. Here are a few examples that Search Institute has
found to be true in both urban and suburban communities
around the country.

Based on the percent of teens responding positively to
these community assets:

1. Young people and their parents communicate positively,
    and young people are willing to seek parent's advice
    and counsel: 24%
2. Young people receive support from three or more non-
    parents adults: 41%
3. Young people experience caring neighbors: 34%
4. School provides a caring encouraging environment:
    27%
5. Parents are actively involved in helping young people
    succeed in school: 27%
6. Young people perceive that adults in the community
    value youth: 19%
7. Young people are given useful roles in the community:
    28%
8. Young people feel safe at home, school, and in the
    neighborhood: 28%
9. Parents and other adults model positive, responsible
    behavior: 28%

Could there possibly be a more unappreciated, unloved,
disconnected and underutilized group in our society? We
wonder why so many teenagers today are hurting and angry.
In this time in history when perhaps the whole culture is flying by the seat of its collective pants, we lay forth for you
our vision of how to reconnect with our teenagers; how to
support our teens in staying grounded; how we can best nurture our relationships with our teens even as we are all fly-

ing by the seat of our black, baggy pants. So the following are our "Baker's Dozen Ways to Relate To Your Teenager". These are ways we can meet their developmental, behavioral and emotional needs.

A Baker's Dozen Ways to Relate To Your Teenager
1. Respect their ideas and feelings.

Be willing to get in their shoes and to see and understand the world from their point of view. The prayer of St. Francis holds the line, "Seek first to understand, then to be understood." This is especially true when relating with teenagers. You do not have to agree with them. Just be willing to get out of your world and into theirs in order to be able to validate their feelings.

2. Do not enter their room without their permission.

Teens need lots of private, quiet time to think, to get clear about things, to talk to their friends. They need to feel safe enough to pour their hearts out into their journals and poetry and artwork and music without worrying that someone (like their parents) will be snooping around their room looking for their secrets.

3. Do not enter their relationships without their permission.

They aren't privy to the nitty-gritty goings on between you and your spouse or your friends, and they need this same kind of space with their relationships. Above all, never ever, ever, criticize or negatively judge their friends. In a sense, most teens feel like they are their friends. When you negatively judge their friends and you do not want to spend time with their friends, you are in their minds judging them and do not want to spend time with them.

4. Respect their space.

There are times when teens want to be with us, so drop everything and run with it. Many times they do not want to be seen within 10 miles of us, so respect that as well. Do not take it personally; it really is not about us.

5. Give more control, power, and "say-so".

Research shows that the results of teens not getting enough say-so at home is decreased motivation, decreased school performance, increased anger and depression, and more acting out. Listen to their needs a lot and give as much control as is reasonable to them. They will learn more from their own successes and mistakes out in the world than they will from our lectures.

6. Agreements and accountability vs. rules and consequences.

Create win-win agreements with them, giving them a lot of say-so about how their life looks and operates. Be sure everyone is clear about the agreements and has bought in. Then be sure to follow through in a kind but firm way no matter what. Holding them accountable to agreements is a great long term gift both to them and you. Stay out of the business of you making the rules, passing them down to your subjects (your teenagers), and then using punishments for motivation. It rarely works with teens and creates major unnecessary power struggles.

7. Have fun with them!

Listen to their music, go to their movies with them. When invited, "hang" with them and their friends. Their world is fascinating. Their energy is fun, free, idealistic, and spontaneous. All the things most adults could use more of you can find in a teenager if you look. Do not miss out, they are only teenagers for a short while.

8. Walk your talk!

There is little that riles up teenagers more than adults with double standards. If you do not want your 16-year-old drinking and driving, then do not have a glass of wine before you go out for the evening. They are watching us like hawks. Practice what you preach. Be in integrity with whatever you are asking of them. It is a great way to show teenagers respect.

9. Respect and love yourself.

They learn best how to take care of themselves by watching how we take care of ourselves. How well is your life balanced? Are you putting your heart and soul into work that you love? Do you eat healthy, exercise regularly? Do you nurture your friendships? Do you take time for spiritual growth?

10. Respect and love your spouse.

Again, as they embark on the journey of special, close intimate relationships, they will lean heavily upon what they have seen at home. Have you shown them peaceful conflict resolution? Do they see a fun and affectionate relationship? Is there cooperation and mutual respect? Do you give of yourself but also not lose yourself in the relationship? Is there kind but firm boundaries in your marriage? Have they seen a committed, loving respectful relationship that grows over time? They deserve to have experienced all of this and more.

11. You reap what you sow!

If you want more respect from your teen, give him or her more respect. Whatever you are demanding of or from them, first look and be sure you are giving it in abundance. That goes for love, time, respect, trust, or whatever. I do not think they should have to earn our love or respect. You can take responsibility for any lack of love or respect in your relationship with your teen and give it to them unconditionally tenfold. That goes against some of our old paradigms, but you truly will reap what you sow with teenagers.

12. Love and accept them for exactly who they are!

Honor their differences. See through their exteriors (hair, tattoos, baggy pants) and do not judge a book by its cover. Beneath all that "stuff" is the same cuddly, warm, funny little kid you used to wrestle with and hold on your lap just a few short years back. There is still a lot of "little kid" in our teens. Make it safe enough for those funny, playful, vulnerable parts of them to come out and play. Teenagers in our culture are judged so negatively today without most adults ever taking the time to get to know them. Smile at them, look for their unique spirit. Let them know that you believe in them and their future despite some "bumps in the road" of their teen years. A 1982 study of 160,000 high school seniors asked the question, "What do you want most in life?" The overwhelming number one response was "I just want to be loved." Love them unconditionally.

13. Have Fun!

Let the awkward, spontaneous, goofy, funny, idealistic, adventurous, sensual teen come out in you. Think about this. What if the world were run by teenagers? Wouldn't we be a lot better off? Enjoy the ride with your teen. You'll never have one like it again!

The most important factor in how much cooperation and how much influence you have with your teens is the state of your relationship with them. This relationship can be called the "Goodwill Account" (See chapter 3). What a goodwill account means is how does our relationship with our teens feel? Is it safe, loving, respectful, trusting and close? Are you adding regular "deposits" to the account by having special time with them, listening to them, validating their feelings, respecting them. empowering them; or are you making withdrawals from the account by not listening, yelling, punishing, blaming or disrespecting them?

If you have taken the time to invest in the relationship, and the goodwill account is full, then it is easy to sit down as in number six above, and work out win-win agreements and then follow through.  You have the ability to have a positive influence on their lives because they will not be afraid to come to you and use you to brainstorm or be a sounding board. They will know you have understanding ears. They will be in a space to listen to some of

There is still a lot of little kid in teenagers.

your wisdom and experience. Despite their sometimes surly or "I don't care" external appearance, teens do need us. Perhaps more than ever before in their lives, they need us. Our involvement has to look differently than it previously did.

It is important to use the "Baker's Dozen" list at times when everyone seems so rushed and stressed out. Do not forget about the special needs of your teenagers and the special skills needed to stay connected to them. Let us work together to change the current feelings that teenagers are awful and that during those teen years the parents and teens must separate and dislike each other. Do not buy into the theory that you should be disconnected until some magical moment when they turn 20. Both teenagers and their parents want closeness and love from each other so try not to just wish for it. Go for it!

Chapter 16
You've Got To Have God

One of the greatest ways to keep your kids grounded is to give them some solid ground to grow from. This is where the importance of religion comes in. A good religious background teaches a child faith and patience and it also gives them a set of rules and guidelines to live by. The Ten Commandments are the best set of rules a child can have. They were handed down from God and maybe there are times when a child will not obey their parents, but one with a good spiritual background will certainly obey God.

Have A Good Church Life
A good church life can mean different things to differ-

ent people. If just going to church is important to you, then you should begin taking your children at an early age. Most churches have "cry rooms" or nurseries or some place for the children to go. Many churches welcome the sweet sounds of young children right into their congregations. Jesus, after all, did say "Let the children come to me."

Besides just attending church, as the children get older, it is helpful to find a Sunday School or a youth group or other smaller groups where the children can meet friends of similar backgrounds. There are often social activities at the church like dinners, picnics and other things that the whole family can attend together. Usually they do not cost much money and can be a fun source of family entertainment.

There are places a teen can fit in at church and also leadership positions he or she can take on. This helps them prepare for the future and gives them a stable place in the world. If a little girl goes to Sunday School each week, she will make friends, and as she grows up those friends may still be there in the youth group. Maybe if they live near the church the friendships will carry over to school or their neighborhood. After she grows up and moves to another town for college, she may seek out a church which may help keep her grounded during those turbulent college years. The harbor of a church can often provide a needed anchor.

Teach Your Children To Pray

In this hectic world, it is important to find some quiet time every day. Praying is a way to meditate and find peace. Teaching your child to pray is a wonderful gift you can give them. If you are a reserved person and have never been raised in a family that prays together, you can overcome that. One of the most rewarding times a family can have is praying together. A simple way to pray together is to have one parent start out with a short prayer and go around the circle and each person may add something. If you choose not to say anything, you can say, "pass". If a parent is noticing a child is never saying anything, it would be ok to say, "try to say something, even if it is just 'thank you God.'" and soon they will be saying something.

There is really no right or wrong way to pray because it is between you and your God. The best way to start out is to thank Him for all the blessings He has given you. By teaching your children to thank God before asking for things, you will teach them to value what they have. Even in times of trouble, there are so many things you can thank God for. This will also teach your child to be optimistic and look for the good in things rather than only seeing the problems.

When your children are young you can gather them together and teach them to pray like this. You can start, "Thank you God for all of the wonderful blessings you have given us. We will now tell you what we are thankful for. I am thankful for the beautiful day we had today..." And then the other adult, if there is one could add, "I am thankful we are all here together," and then it is the child's turn. When they are young and just learning to pray out loud you may get anything and you have to try not to laugh. You could get "thank you God for my new Legos," and to that you can add, "That was very good, it feels good to thank God for all our blessings. Another thing you can thank God for is that He gave you eyes to see your Legos and healthy hands to play with them."

Sometimes a prayer is good at a family meeting, or maybe you hold "home church" when you are unable to go to church. Sometimes it is just fun to have a family devotional. These things may seem strange to you if you have never done them, but they open the lines of communication up within a family. If you can actually talk about your greatest fears and concerns, things you would talk to God about, you are really communicating.

As the children get older, let them lead the prayers. Tell your oldest son ahead of time that he will be leading the prayer today and he can think of what to say. Most of the time they will be proud to be able to do it. Another way to promote praying out loud is during dinner. Rather than say the usual grace (which grounded, healthy families often start their meals

Teaching your children to pray can be a wonderful gift.

with, whether out loud or to themselves) occasionally have one of the children lead the family in grace. Besides helping them pray, it also promotes confidence. If you can pray out loud, which is a very personal thing, you will be able to speak to a group. It is an important and helpful skill for a kid to learn while growing up.

Teach Your Child To Use The Bible

Even if you are not a regular Bible reader, you can give your child a good biblical background. Have Bibles be a part of their everyday life from babyhood. There are bible poem books for toddlers, then children's bibles with beautiful pictures. These would be good for bedtime stories. Youth Bibles are good and stories can be pulled out of them for family devotional or home church Sundays. When your child is old enough, make sure he has a Bible of his own. Encourage him to keep his Bible by his bed and if he is ever afraid in the night, he can turn on his light and read from it, or at least take the Bible into his bed and sleep with it. This teaches the Bible as a source of security. Pack the Bible in his overnight bag when he goes on a trip to Grandma and Grandpa's, camping or anyplace else. You do not even have to encourage reading the Bible on these trips, it is just getting him in the routine of always taking his Bible.

Your child will decide for herself if she is going to read the Bible, but you are providing the groundwork. Teach her to use it for comfort as well as a source of joy. Show her a few key verses like the 23rd Psalm and others so that if she ever needs them she will know where to find them. Teach her a respect for the Bible, but also show her you can write the verses in the front or underline them if you want to remember something. By writing in your Bible you are personalizing it and it becomes more of a friend to you.

Family and Spirituality Go Hand In Hand

In order to be the best family member you can be, you have to have a foundation on which *you* stand. You cannot teach a child to have a well-grounded life unless you are firmly entrenched in one yourself. Many times we are more grounded than we think we are. Even though things can become so topsy turvy in our everyday lives, make sure you nurture your children's spirituality. It will become a life long legacy that you have passed on to them.

Chapter 17
Keeping Traditions Alive

Doesn't it seem like things just get more hectic about the time you need them to slow down? Take for instance, the winter holidays. Whether you celebrate Christmas, Hanukkah, Kwanza, or another holiday, you probably envision happy times spent with your family. Those same feelings arise when you think of planning your child's birthday, First Holy Communion, Bar Mitzvah or whatever. In reality, those times seem to be the most busy. There are gifts to buy, the house must be cleaned up for guests, and many other activities which surround these events take place, generally causing you to feel more busy and crabby than ever. It does not have to be that way if you'd not let it.

Birthdays

Remember why it is that you are celebrating your child's birthday. It is a celebration of his or her life. It should not be a time to compete with "the Joneses." These days people are going to so much trouble and expense for their children's birthdays, when all the youngsters really want is to know someone cared enough to celebrate it with them.

A little planning ahead can make all the difference in the world. Start traditions for your children's birthdays and then live up to them. Maybe you like to cook, so ask your child what he wants for his birthday. Buy that ahead of time so that on the day of the birthday, you can be prepared and spend time with your child, but also cook the special meal. Some people prefer having the child choose a favorite restaurant to go out to. You might want to set boundaries as far as the choices. Have the child choose the restaurant the week before so that when the big day arrives, you all know what to expect.

Birthday Parties

If you get into the habit of trying to give your child the biggest and best party you are sending the wrong message. You may also be adding to your own stress. Now, there are some par-

Birthday parties are a favorite tradition for kids.

ties, which although they cost more, might save you some trouble, and if you can afford that type, you could try them. An example of this would be to hire one of those clowns who puts on the parties. Sometimes you can find one that is reasonable and they basically do it all. People who go all out and get pony rides or cooking classes just to give their child the best party will have a problem because next year they will not be able to top it.

One good idea is to limit the parties. Suggest every other year the child gets a party with friends and on the odd year, you just spend it with the family. An old-fashioned birthday party with cake and ice cream and games is still a hit with children. They do not need to be entertained with all of the fancy extras; they enjoy just running around playing with their friends. You should think about your child and then think about what type of party to have. If your daughter is a big horse lover and reads books about horses all the time, maybe it would be fun to go to a ranch to ride horses or have pony rides. This can be costly, so if you want to do something big like that, maybe just take a cousin or sibling. Children do not always need big numbers at their party. As long as they feel special, that is all that matters.

If funds are a problem, you can be creative. Let us say that your daughter who loves horses wants a horse theme party but you can not afford ponies—make a cake in the shape of a horse's head (very simple) and a horse piñata.

Party Ideas
Horse Head Cake

Bake an inexpensive yellow cake using one round cake pan and one square one. The round one will be the head. Cut part of the square one into a smaller square and set it at the 4:00 position to your round one. Take the remaining part of the cake and make pointed ears (put them at the 11:00 position) and a neck (about 7:00 and 8:00)

Horse Piñata

Piñatas are a fun addition to any party. They are easy and inexpensive to make, or you can buy one at a party store. Blow up two balloons: one large one and one small one. The large one is the body, the small one is the head. Use paper towel or toilet paper rolls for the legs and neck. To make ears, be creative, pile newspaper and cover it with masking tape to form two little pointed ears. Now that you have your structure made, cut newspapers into inch-thick strips. Dip the strips in a solution of paste made from cornstarch, flour and water or just flour and water. Make the paste very thin. Dip the paper in, and wrap it around the structure until it is fully covered. Make the belly part thick enough, but not too thick. Dry it on a pile of newspapers. The next day, spray paint it with brown paint and decorate as you wish. Your child may even want to add yarn down the back for the mane. This could be a fun activity you do with your child. Do it enough ahead of time that it does not interfere with your "day before the party" chores.

Home Made Magician

Another inexpensive way to have a party is to invite "The Great Dadini!" (or "Mommini"). This is the world renowned magician, who is also known as mom. Here's how to do it:

Learn a few tricks, first of all. Do not tell your child what you have planned. When it comes to the part in your party where you want to have the magic show, have the children sit down. Tell them you have a big surprise for them. Make a grand announcement that ends it with "I present to you the Great Dadini!" Then walk out and put on a hat and walk back with your tricks. Have a table sitting nearby which you can use and be sure the children are far enough back they will not see your tricks. Here are a few simple tricks you can do to "amaze" your audience.

Disappearing Scarf Trick

Take a brown lunch bag. Cut the front out of it and stick it down into another bag of the same size. Glue the ends and bottom down. Now you have what looks like a lunch bag, but it has a "trap" door inside of it. Your "scarf" should be a small piece of scrap material. As you hold the bag up for your audience, you hold the inside bag against the outside bag so that it just looks like one bag. Show your audience the scarf.

"I will now place the scarf in the bag," you say as you put it in the bag, which is the inside bag. With your other hand, you grab the bag and tilt it towards you so they can not see it as you open it, you grab the center and hold it towards the other side, which now opens the "secret trap door." Act like you are trying to pour the scarf out of the bag.

"Hey, where did my scarf go?" you ask as you quickly show them it is empty. Just as quickly, close it back up again and then tap the bag three times.

"Maybe if you all helped me out on this one," you say. "Now on the count of three yell, 'come back you scarf!'"

Miraculously as they yell "come back you scarf" the scarf appears. What you have done is switched hands again and grasped the other side so the part with the scarf in it is showing. Your audience will be amazed!

The Four Aces Card Trick

This is one most grown-ups know and many older kids know, but the younger crowd usually enjoys it. Take a deck of cards. Have three random cards followed by the four aces. Here's what you say:

This deck of cards is a building. The four aces are the bank robbers. See here they are: (and show them the aces real fast, keeping the other three cards in place and hidden). The head robber tells his friends: 'you go to the first floor (and you take the top card—which is not an ace, remember, it is any old card), and the second guy, 'you go to the middle floor (put that somewhere in the deck, again, it is not an ace.) The third ace he tells to go to an upper floor (and you put that card in somewhere near the top. Now you have gotten rid of the three random cards and the four aces are still left.) I will stay on guard at the top of the building and when I see the police coming I will signal you like this (thump, thump, thump, you tap the top of the deck) and all of you aces should come to the top. (as you are saying that, turn over the four aces and watch your audience's looks of delight).

Cookie Decorating Party

If you plan a party around a theme, you can be creative. Younger children enjoy taking a sugar cookie and decorating it with icing and sprinkles. This could be eaten in place of a birthday cake and you could put a candle in your child's cookie.

Another version of this type of party would be make your own ice cream sundaes, and who does not like to make their own sundae!

Make Your Own Pizza Party

This can be fun for a pre-teen who still wants to have a birthday party but wants to have a more grown up gathering. You can be as creative as you want to with the invitations. One suggestion is to go to a pizza place and ask if you can have or buy some small pizza boxes. Have your son or daughter make "pizzas" out of construction paper and then "deliver" them to the prospective guests. The pizzas would be the invitation with the information about where and when the party will be held. They could each bring a topping or bring the toppings they want, or you could furnish many different toppings. For busy parents, you can just pick up the individual sized ready-made pizza crusts they sell in the grocery stores. If you have the time or desire, you can add "tossing" the pizza to the party and each kid could be given a ball and they can actually make their own. While the pizza is cooking, girls can be doing each other's hair and nails, with supplies furnished by you; or the boys could be trading sports cards or playing electronic games.

Other Birthday Suggestions

Some people have special traditions for birthdays and here are just a few you might want to try:

The Birthday Story

Each year at sometime on the child's birthday, sit him or her down and tell the "birthday story." This is the story of what was going on the day they were born. It might start like this. "Daddy and I had each other and we loved each other very much. We decided we wanted someone to share that love with

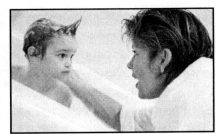

Kids love to hear about the day they were born

so we asked God for you. Seven years ago this very day, you came, and it was the happiest day of our lives. We were at a party and I started feeling kind of funny. Daddy drove me to the hospital. When we got to the car we found we had a flat tire, so we had to call grandma and she came to get us..." Everyone has a story about the day their children were born. If it is the second or third child or wherever it falls, add something like, "We had so much love we wanted to spread it around," or "we wanted to bring a sister for your brother to play with." If you remember to tell the birthday story every year it will become a fun family tradition that is expected and anticipated.

Measuring Your Child's Height

Some people like to measure their child and record it on their birthday. If you are in a home you plan to stay in the rest of your life, you could do it on a basement wall or garage wall, or even the inside of a closet or closet door. The other alternative is to make your own growth chart or buy one and mark the height each birthday. If you do it at a special time like right before the cake or something, it will become something everyone looks forward to doing each year.

Doing something fun and special for your child's birthday and saving it on video will help you remember it forever.

Birthday Book

Another nice way to record a special day and make it memorable is to have a birthday book. Each year you can add pictures and information. On your child's birthday, it is fun to go back and look at previous birthdays.

Birthday Video

Why not take the video you may have used when your child was born and save it. Each year, add a little to it, to get a chronological look at your child. On the child's birthday, after taking the video of that birthday, it will be nice to look at the other birthdays on the tape. This just reinforces to the child the continuity of love and support they have had over the years.

No matter what you do for your child's birthday, just try to take some time out of your schedule for some planning to make it special. One birthday here or there where you rush to McDonalds and buy a store-bought cake all in the same day, may be the best you can do that year, but really trying to make birthdays special will contribute to that stable, happy childhood we are all striving to give our children.

Holidays

Try to remember some of the special traditions you celebrated when you were a child and incorporate them into your family's holidays. If it is a religious holiday and you are particularly busy, try to find the time to have small devotionals or other family gatherings where you talk about the true meaning of the holiday. If your family is Jewish, take the time to play the Dreidel game. It is simple and does not take long. Observe the candle lighting of Hanukkah and all of the other things that make it meaningful to you. If you are Christian, try getting an advent wreath or calendar. Advent calendars can be nice because each day you open a door and talk about something briefly, then there is usually a prize or a piece of candy. Some families enjoy having weekly devotionals during Advent. Try to take the focus off of the big presents that they see advertised on television.

Another way to observe a holiday is by helping others.

Teach your children the importance of volunteerism by making placemats or cards for a hospital or retirement home. Volunteer at a soup kitchen or homeless shelter, or help your children get a clothing drive started and take the items in together.

Chapter 18
Slow Down, You're Moving Too Fast!
(You've Got To Make Your Family Last!)

Everybody today, seems to be in such a terrible rush, anxious for greater developments and greater riches and so on; so that children have very little time for their parents and parents have very little time for each other. And so in the home begins the disruption of the peace of the world.

Mother Theresa of Calcutta

Somehow, someway, we have lost some of the old traditional ways of connecting with our loved ones. Blame it on the Industrial Revolution or urbanization, but the fact of the matter is that we as a culture have lost the ability to have fun and do more with less. We have lost the ability to enjoy the slower, simpler pleasures of life. We have been conditioned to need quick sound bites of fun or immediate gratification. When our computers take 10 seconds to spit forth their information, we become impatient and frustrated. We need to be constantly entertained and stimulated at high intensity levels. Because of this, we are missing out on a lot of vintage moments and experiences: moments of closeness and wonder.

The following are some examples of activities and experiences that you can bring back for your family, to strengthen your connections to each other and with your pasts. Despite your already overloaded schedule, once you become involved in these activities you may realize you have more time than you first thought. These things help our children learn the value and magic of watching things grow from a seed over weeks and months; they help us watch constellations slowly drift across the sky from season to season (or clouds from minute to minute); they help us watch birds from the onset of nest-building through the egg stage to a mature bird. We help our children (and ourselves) notice and appreciate the passing of time, seasons, cycles of nature; to learn to relax and smell the roses (and plant some too!); to experience the security and good feelings that come from being a part of family traditions. This chapter was one of our favorites to write.

1. Gardening

When was the last time you planted something from seed? Today we are in too big a rush to wait for seeds to grow. We buy plants. Every grocery store you go into has bedding plants already in bloom in the early spring. It is so convenient, you do not even have to go to a nursery.

Whether you buy seeds or plants, it is good to involve your children in the process. Remember their joy when they brought home the seed in the Styrofoam cup, when they were younger. Recapture that wonder and delight in your own backyard.

Take your children to the nursery and have them pick out flowers or trees, vegetables or whatever they want to plant. Have them read all

It's fun to get involved in something like gardening with yor child.

of the information about when to sow the seeds, how to care for them, whether the plant needs full sun or partial sun, etc. Sometimes an advisor like a grandma or grandpa or an elderly neighbor helps.

The pleasure derived from the weeding and watering and especially watching the plants grow is experienced over weeks and months as opposed to the minutes it takes to buy a plant. If you do choose to buy plants, teach your children about pinching off the wilted blooms and watering the plant, and trimming it. Waiting for perennials to re-emerge and bloom gives kids a sense of their long-term gift to the world and they are so proud when they can give people flowers, carrots, tomatoes or anything else they have grown. There is something very relaxing about watering flowers on a hot summer evening.

After dinner, before dark, is a glorious time of day to spend in your yard with your family. There just seems to be a certain calm and peace that you do not feel at any other time of day.

If you have a favorite woodland area or a farm, consider digging up a sapling and replanting it in your yard.

My family re-planted two silver maples and three white pines from my wife Anne's parent's farm. Even though they sold the farm seven years ago, the five trees are a living monument to those memories of the fun times they had at Gramma and Grandpa's farm. There really is a lot of wonder involved when you can look up at a 25 foot tree towering over your two story house and remember it as the five foot high sapling that you transplanted just seven years ago.

T. J.

As a child, flowers played a big part in my family's leisure time. My parents enjoyed taking the family for drives to look at the Dogwoods when they were in bloom. Grandma had a beautiful garden of irises, which she proudly took you to see when they were out. My husband, Rob's grandmother also raised irises and when she moved, we dug up some of her white irises and planted them in our yard. When my grandparents passed away we dug up some of their purple ones. My grandfather's brother -in -law sent me some that he had grown, and a friend of my grandpa gave me some of hers. Now Rob and I and our two sons anxiously wait for the first iris to bloom in the spring. It is a wonderful reminder of the simpler times I used to experience as a child and a way to get my children to have the same fond feelings about gardens and springtime and their relations.

S.T. R.

2. Stargazing

Two summers ago, the Jordan family along with our friends and their three kids (six kids and four adults total) drove out to Colorado for a vacation. The first night was spent camping out in the mountains along a white water river on a gorgeous, clear evening. One of the parents invited the children to come lay down on the rocks by the river to look for shooting stars. He was met with looks of disbelief and boredom, but he went anyway. A short time later, he was joined by the other parents. Finally, one by one, the five children, ages 8-16, sauntered down to the river until all 10 of them were lying on sleeping bags stargazing as you can only do when high up in the mountains. About every five minutes or so they would see a shooting star. It was one of the most relaxing, peaceful and fun times of the ten day vacation. Everyone enjoyed a much richer show than anything they could have watched on television or a computer screen.

T. J.

Because my husband is a baseball writer, every year we are lucky enough to get to go to Spring Training—our favorite place has been St. Petersburg, Fla. We would take the two boys down and my parents came, and for years my grandpa also made the trip. The nights would be so warm and beautiful and grandpa would point out Orion, The Hunter, because he is up there in the night skies of March, and other constellations. To this day, we look for Orion in the winter and think fondly of those great nights.

S. T. R.

What better way to slow down and unwind at the end of

a hectic day than to sit outside and try to find the Big Dipper or Orion or Pegasus. You do not have to be an astronomer to enjoy the night skies with your family. Go to the library or bookstore and pick up book about the stars. Because our earth and solar system are constantly moving, the skies look different at different times of the year.

The Basics On The Constellations

Many years ago people gave imaginative names to groups of stars or constellations. As the ancient peoples looked into the skies they saw a lion, a bull, a dragon and a mighty archer. They gave names to them: the lion they called Leo; the bull was Taurus; the Dragon was Draco; and Orion was the hunter.

There are 88 constellations in all and even though many people think the Big Dipper is a con-

Learning about things like constellations is another way to connect with your child.

stellation, it is not. The Big Dipper is part of a constellation called The Big Bear, or Ursa Major. This is one of the easiest constellations for people, especially children to find; and the Big Dipper is easy to pick out. The handle of the dipper is also the tail of the bear.

After you have located the Big Dipper it is easy to find the North Star by finding the two stars that form the front of the Big Dipper's cut. After you have found them look at an imaginary line at the bottom star going up ward. The brightest star you come to will be the North Star. The North Star helps you find other things. It is the first star in the handle of the Little Dipper (Ursa Minor), which is also fun for children to find. If you can find the North Star, you will be able to orient yourself with North, South, East, and West.

Orion is another commonly found constellation. It is easy to spot because there are three fairly bright stars right in a row which form the belt of the hunter. Once you find the belt you can imagine the hunter up there holding his bow.

Toss a blanket on the ground and take your kids outside. It's an exciting show with stories of heroes and adventure and it is all free and right in your own backyard.

3. Cloud Dissipation Game

As long as you and the kids are looking up, how about some old fashion cloud-gazing? When was the last time you laid down on a hillside and looked for pictures in the clouds? Play the Cloud Dissipation game. Gather your clan together and find a cloud for everyone to stare at. See if by pooling your "psychic efforts" you can make that cloud dis-

appear, dissolve. "Buh bye cloud." It is a great way to add to the enjoyment of a sunset.

4. Campfires

Who does not enjoy a good campfire? Staring at the fire, roasting marshmal-lows, making "s'mores,"

Campfires offer many ways to share with your children.

singing campfire songs or telling stories. Little kids and big ones too love to get a stick in their hands and poke and prod the wood and coals. Gathering the wood can even be a great adventure. Most cities have parks or campground areas to enjoy a good blaze. If not, then create the next best thing in your own backyard.

Outdoor fireplaces can be bought at your local hardware stores allowing you to have a legal campfire at home. It will attract neighborhood kids and adults alike. While you are enjoying the fire, why not create a story-telling tradition. Everyone can recite their favorite scary stories or family stories or animal stories. Create a tradition for a certain holiday or first day of summer. These are the memories kids will hang onto forever.

We lived in Scottsdale, Ariz. for a year, and on cool nights, our friends would invite us over and have a fire in their fire pot (also called a Mexican chiminea). These times of friendship and family were so special to us that we bought a fire pot at a pottery store the day we moved home, and we enjoy having fires in our backyard.

S. T. R.

5. Bird Watching

With the first hint of spring, we see the robin fluttering around, but do you still take the time to watch? It can be joyful thing to experience with your children, the various birds in your own backyard.

I bought two birdfeeders and I built one two years ago. The kids and I have been fascinated by all of the different kinds of visitors we find in the feeders. The variety of birds necessitated a trip to the library and looking up bird books. This has involved the whole family and has been a lot of fun.

T. J.

There are quite a variety of books with good pictures in them to help you identify birds. Feeding them throughout the winter gives everyone in your family a sense of giving. Watching the birds hatch from eggs is another fun gift from birdfeeders. It is fun to sit quietly on the porch and watch the birds fly in and out. There are times in your busy day that you deserve some short relaxing time. If you have a comfortable place outside on a patio or just some lawn chairs in the backyard, you can ask one of your kids to join you. Sometimes if your children are occupied doing something else, you could go out yourself and if you see a particularly glorious cardinal, call enthusiastically in to them and they will probably share your excitement when they come out into the yard and see the bird. Bird watching can be very relaxing.

Make A Bird Feeder

If you want to see a variety of birds, put out a bird feeder and keep it filled with bird seed. Certain types of seeds bring certain types of birds. There are stores which carry many brands of bird feeders. You can make simple ones with your children, hang them up outside, and wait for the hungry birds to come.

A pine cone bird feeder
Take a pine cone and fill it with either suet or peanut butter. Hang it on a tree upside down by a string.

Taking a walk in a nature park can bring a family closer. It's even more special with grandparents.

Hanging bird feeder
Another way to make a birdfeeder is to

attach string to a coffee can, plastic tub, or coconut shell and hang it from a tree. Fill the container with birdseed, peanut butter, suet, fruit or bread crumbs. It is fun to get a book to help you identify the birds and keep a record of the birds you see. Your children will delight in being able to identify the birds on their own, with you there watching, of course.

6. Nature Hikes

So far all of the suggestions in this chapter have involved being out in nature. This was not by accident. Mary Pipher, author of <u>The Shelter of Each Other</u>, notes that research shows that the three things adults remember most fondly about growing up are family vacations, family dinners together and family time in nature. Find some good walking or hiking trails in your area and have at it. Taking walks around the block in your neighborhood are also a nice way of meeting your neighbors.

Parks and forests do a great job of creating different levels of hiking paths. Many of the paths are paved and they even have maps to help you find your way. Make sure everyone gets a good walking stick. Explore every creek bed you come across. Swing on a vine if you feel safe doing

Sharing nursery rhymes is a dradition handed down from generation to generation.

it. Climb on and over fallen trees. Look on the ground at the wildflowers and try to identify them. Look for animal tracks. Children love to collect things on nature walks, so it might be fun to bring a plastic sack along. Have a blast.

7. Nursery Rhymes

Because kids are spending so much time today watching videos and playing computer games, singing and reciting nursery rhymes often gets left behind. We think it is important to share these handed-down treasures. There was a lot of closeness and value in repeatedly singing those songs and verses. The continuity gives children a sense of security and safety. What better way to snuggle up under the blanket than with a Mother Goose book! They are great for helping your children learn memorization, learn words, learn to read. They are another excellent way to create those memories of fun and closeness.

Nursery rhymes also give way to poetry. For young children, read nursery rhymes; and as the children grow older, it is good to continue with poems they might enjoy, such as "Casey at the Bat," "The Night Before Christmas," and "Winken, Blynken and Nod." Eugene Field has some great transitional poems that sound like nursery rhymes.

My grandma used to recite "Little Boy Blue" to us quite often. She would get the whole family around and start, "The little toy dog was covered with rust, but sturdy and staunch he stands..." With no effort at all, everyone in my family knows that poem by heart. It would take a little more effort to memorize "Paul Revere's Ride," but when my grandma was very ill, my grandpa decided to memorize it to take his mind off of his problems. When he was in his 70's he memorized it. He also used to recite some great Robert Service and Edgar Guest Poems. It has been a tradition in my family, almost like story telling, to hand down poems from generation to generation, and it all starts with nursery rhymes.

S. T. R.

Some of Our Favorite Nursery Rhymes
This Little Piggy
Hey Diddle Diddle
Mary Had A Little Lamb
Diddle Diddle Dumpling
Humpty Dumpty
Rock A Bye Baby
What are yours?

---

8. Family Traditions

If you had traditions as a child, carry them on with your new family. Some families had taffy pulls, made home-made ice cream (with each member taking a turn at cranking it), some made piles with the leaves in the autumn and jumped in them. Whatever your family did that brings back warm, fuzzy feelings for you, do the same for your children when they are growing up. For the busiest of families, it may take some planning, but pick a date and stick with it.

My wife, Anne's family has had a Christmas family reunion every year for 106 years. Her parents both grew up in a small farming community in rural Missouri. One of the ways they raise the money for the Christmas feast is through their annual apple-butter cooking.

Relatives from newborns through people in their 90's show up at dawn to peel apples and start the fire and all day long the apple butter has to be constantly stirred to keep it from burning. It really does take a village to raise apple butter! The children contribute. They get to be involved in and experience a process that takes all day to perform. They see the 90 year old great grandma being helped to the pot. She tastes the apple butter and instructs the group as to what needs to be added or how much more time it will take.

It is truly a multi-generational endeavor. At the end of the cooling process, the applebutter is poured into pint and quart jars to be sold to raise money for the holiday get together.

T. J.

It is good for kids to be involved in such traditions that connect them to their heritage. It also allows them to connect with the "elders" in their family and receive some of their wisdom and blessings. It is another one of those family times where everyone feels valuable and close.

My dad was raised on a ranch in Oklahoma. He used to ride a pony, shoot at pesky coyotes who threatened the ranch, and do many things that my sisters and I, who were raised in a city never dreamed of doing on a daily basis. He told us stories of what it was like back then, and he taught us how to use a lariat. Ever since we were kids we knew how to "lasso," and since we have grown and some of us have children, we have passed that tradition on. My dad made each of the grandchildren his or her own lasso and taught them how to use it. We've always made sure to take them to the rodeo whenever we see one nearby, and every summer they take horseback riding lessons. Though they live in a big city, my boys will always have a little cowboy in them from their "papa."

S.T.R.

With families moving so often these days, you may not live near your family. If that is the case you may need to start some new ones of your own. Bread baking is a good one, as is making candy apples.

For years, our family has bought white ceramic snow village pieces and painted them to give as gifts to teachers or relatives. We love the feeling of the five of us sitting around the kitchen table all painting to our hearts delight. We are all very proud when we display our "favorites" during the Christmas holidays. What started out as a few houses on a card table now fills up a large folding table. We add new houses and stores and decorations every year.

T. J.

Start your own traditions that fit your family's interests and personality. Do not put this off, think up some ideas and start today. One of the things we all like so much about traditions is that something about it reminds us of simpler times. For a short while, as we are engaging in it again, we can go back to those earlier times. Sights and smells from your own childhood can influence the ideas you have for creating traditions. If you do not have time to bake bread from scratch (and if you think about it, we could all make the time if we really wanted to), you can buy a bread maker. If you set it up so it will bake the bread over night, the aroma of fresh bread will wake you up and will create a wonderful homey feeling in your house. It takes no time at all and there is such a difference in a family eating fresh bread together—even if it was made in a bread maker.

9. Reading the Classics

Children love to be read to. Try starting a tradition of buying the classic books like <u>Black Beauty</u>, <u>Robinson Crusoe</u> and <u>Treasure Island</u>. Read a chapter or two each night. Browse through used book stores and flea markets to find books that everyone wants to read. Besides instilling in kids the love of reading, it creates a lot more closeness than sitting glued to the television set.

My mother had a wonderful idea for reading to my sisters and me. She would take a book, like <u>The Five Little Peppers and How They Grew,</u>*,* <u>The Bobbsy Twins</u> *or* <u>Little Women</u> *and change the names of the characters and put our names in. I became Meg in* <u>Little Women</u> *and the story seemed to come alive even more for us. She has a very special voice and can really read a story.*

On some nights when my mom was not reading the story, my dad would announce that he had seen his friend "P.J." sometime during the day and he would tell us about it after we got into bed. "P.J. Potts was a friend of Peter Pans," he would say. And then he would add, "You know, Potts and Pan," and we would all laugh. There was a always some sort of exciting thing that P.J. had told him and he would tell us. To this day, I am not quite sure if P.J. was real or not and that's half the fun. I do know that Pop started running into P.J. again when my sons became old enough to hear a story.

S. T. R.

10. Building Forts, Club Houses, and Play Houses

This is another way to spend great quality time with kids without having to spend any money. The simplest fort can be made by just lying in bed with your child and pulling the covers up over your heads. Pretend to hear bears growling or wolves howling. Occasionally poke your head out to check out the "campsite." Use your imagination.

Another type of your "upscale" fort is the blanket or

sheet fort. You can cover any-thing from a card table to some chairs, desks or couches arranged in a square with the blanket. Half the fun is crawling inside with a flashlight. Kids love to have these special "hide away" places.

If the neighbors are moving, you can use some of their extra boxes, or better yet, if someone gets a new dryer or washer, those big boxes make great forts. The parents can help by cutting out windows and doors. The boxes can be decorated to prolong the fun. After the fun of playing in the playhouse is over, move the cardboard to a

Whether it's a home-made go-cart or one made from a kit for the All American Soap Box Derby, working on a go-cart is a great way for togetherness.

hill in the backyard and tell the kids to take their shoes off and slide down the cardboard in their socks. A "sled" can be made by using a smaller piece of cardboard and taking a running start and then sliding down the long piece of card-board on the smaller piece. You may even find yourself gig-gling along with the kids.

For those really energetic and handy parents, you can find old scrap wood and make club houses or tree houses with hammers and nails. Most of the fun you will have is the time and creativity it takes to make it. Working with your child brings real togetherness. Do not forget to let them take some swipes with the hammer--under good supervision, of course.

11. Make Go-Carts

You can make a simple "go cart" if you have a few pieces of scrap wood and some old wheels. Just use one long piece for the body. At each end, put a cross board and attach wheels on each end of the crossboards. On the front crossboard, you can put a long nail in the center and when you sit on the go-cart you can use your feet to steer it. Put one foot on each side of the front crossboard and if you want to turn right, push your left foot and the car will turn. The simplest things are the most fun. There is no need to get a motor and make it professional. We are talking about doing something with your child that will not take long to make and does not cost a lot. If you do not have a hill to ride down, you may need to push or attach a rope to the front like you would on a sled, and pull. If you have several children or neighborhood friends they can take turns being the puller.

12. Teach Your Kids How To Change A Tire

Pumping gas, changing a tire and checking the oil are all things that everyone should know about. When children go to the gas station they enjoy pumping the gas and paying the attendant. This is a good time to teach your child how to check the oil. Letting your children help you do things at the service station both helps them feel needed and teaches them the life skill of taking care of a car.

How To Change A Tire

Hopefully, when you teach your child how to change a tire it will be on a leisurely day in your own driveway and not at the side of the road. Try to put a wedge under the wheel opposite the tire you are going to change to avoid having the car slip backwards.

Open the trunk and get out the jack. There will probably be instructions for using that specific car's jack, they are different. Pry off the wheel cover first by using the sharp end of the lug wrench which is with the jack. The other end of the wrench is for unscrewing the nuts. First loosen the nuts, then use the jack to lift the car. Lift the car just high enough that the flat tire is above the ground. Take the nuts all the way off. After you get the nuts off you can pull off the wheel. Put the spare tire on and reverse the directions. This is just a simple explanation, you have to read the directions with your own car.

As kids get older, you can teach them to use battery cables to charge a dead battery. This can be dangerous if not done properly so make sure they never do it unsupervised. Let your children know about these things well before they turn 16 so they will be prepared when they get into the car to drive. It is educational and it provides a time of togetherness when you are working on the car.

Chapter 19
Helping Kids Understand Our Changing World

Every night on the 6:00 news it seems there is another story that is inappropriate for the children to hear. Back when you were kids, the worse thing a child had to contend with was the sad stories of the Vietnam war, the scary riots, or the wave of assassinations. These stories are all horrible, but today on a regular basis kids are hearing about coaches who abuse children, teachers who act inappropriately with their students, children killing children, and even our country's leaders becoming involved in huge scandals.

Congresswoman Mary Bono asked the famous question, "What do we tell the children?" during President Bill Clinton's impeachment hearings. We have some ideas on the subject and offer ways you can deal with the situation. We hope they help. Remember to relax. Kids understand things often at much deeper levels than we give them credit for.

The way you live your life is a thousand times more influential than what they read or see on television. If you are living your life in a manner that can have a good positive influence on your children you are aware of what they are watching on the television. You can monitor the news hour if you think your children are too young. With all of the inappropriate news that is going on it is just important that you spend more time trying to keep your own kids grounded. Tend to the weeds in your own garden before you invest any time or energy on your neighbors yard.

Dr. Jordan's Tips On Handling Kids' Questions About President Clinton's Affair

1.   Turn off the television set! Kids below middle school age probably do not need to watch the evening news. Play Monopoly instead. Watching television is different from reading the paper. Children should be encouraged to read the newspaper, but you should guide them. You can select stories for them to read, like the sports or certain stories you think are appropriate for their age. With the newspaper, you can be selective about what your kids see. On the television news, there is no way to know what story will come on next.

2.   Whenever young children ask us questions that make us uncomfortable, it is usually best to turn it back to them with a question. If they ask you what you think about something, you can say "What do you think about that? or "What do you think that means?" This allows you to hear their private logic which tells where they are and what they are really thinking and you can respond at that level.

3. Turn questions about issues like Clinton's affair into an opportunity to reinforce more general principles or values you believe in. For instance, you could say President Clinton had some problems with his wife and he lied about it. Then, like Pinnocchio, he started lying to cover up his lie and his problems got bigger just like Pinnocchio's nose got bigger. Tell them it is always best to be honest and tell the truth up front and be willing to take responsibility for your actions.

4. With older children, ask them what they think about the issue or how they would have handled it. This can open your eyes to where your teens are in forming their own set of values and principles and lead to some great, deep discussions.

5. Avoid judging or criticizing people. Your child may have acted in a similar manner as the people in the news unbeknownst to you. Your judgments could close the door on them seeing you as a safe sounding board. Be open and non-judgmental.

6. Avoid putting public figures on a pedestal in the first place. Bill Clinton and the Pope are regular people just like you and I. It is OK to let your children feel respect and reverence for the Pope and for the office of the president, but remember they are mortals here on earth, they are not God. They make mistakes just like the rest of us. Putting them on a pedestal makes it harder to connect with them at a level that would give us permission to emulate them. Let your kids know that when the Pope was eight years old he went to school and played soccer just like they do. Let your children know they can have an impact on the world just like the Pope or the president have.

Chapter 20
Taking Care of *You*!

Guess what gets placed last on the priority list when you and your family are flying by the seat of your pants? *You.* Taking care of you, and taking care of your marriage are two things which if neglected, can throw every aspect of your life and family out of whack. Let us explore the why's and how-to's of taking care of yourself and your marriage.

First off, let's talk about reasons why we might not be taking good care of ourselves. For some people, it is a deservability issue. Because of low self confidence, they feel everyone else's needs are more important than their own. For others it is a lack of confidence to ask for what they want, especially when it comes to things people could do for them that would be nurturing. Some people have spent so many years pleasing other people and giving up what they want that they do not have a clue as to what they want today. Questions like how can I serve you or nurture you are met with blank stares.

Another reason people do not take care of themselves is because they think they would be acting selfishly. They may have learned this in their family or through other conditioning. They think being a martyr and sacrificing themselves is more appreciated than living in balance. A person may have seen one or both of their parents model a lifestyle where they did not take the time to take care of themselves.

There are some children growing up who get their value and love from taking care of everyone else and disregarding their own needs. Perhaps they were made to feel guilty whenever they asked for something or did something for themselves. The end result of these and other examples is the belief that taking care of yourself is negative or bad, and so it is no wonder that adults who grew up in this belief system end up placing self-care at the bottom of their lists.

Anyone with children, young or old, has experienced that huge dose of reality that there are *always* things to be done. There always diapers to be changed, noses to be wiped, dirty clothes to be washed, groceries to be bought, sibling fights to be handled, parent-teacher conferences to be attending, party treats to be made, carpools to be driven, friends to be picked up, baseball games to watch, curfews to be negotiated, prom queens to be made up. Whew! Life is full of certainties as well as surprises when you have children of all sizes and ages. There are costs to you and your spouse and the kids when you neglect to take care of some very important people: the cook, cleaner, chauffeur, mediator, nurse, launderer and perpetual fans in your home: *you.*

What Are The Costs Of Neglecting Your Own Needs?

Costs you say, what costs? How about exhaustion. Whether you are a stay-at-home parent or parent who works outside of the home, you will need energy and patience in order to be effective with your parenting. We all do. Our mood sets the tone for the entire house. If you have not been taking care of yourself, it is very easy to feel depleted, and tired. With this exhaustion comes feelings of anger and resentment. We tend to blame others for our lot. We get more impatient and crabby and are much more apt to bark and lash out at our loved ones for less and less serious infractions.

It becomes harder and harder to dredge up the energy to play baseball in the yard, or read those last few books at bedtime without falling asleep half way through. Even if you do make the effort to spend the time with your child, if you are tense or restless, your child will feel it. Parents who are too tired become more distracted and distant and when kids experience this in their parents they feel disconnected. They react in some way to their parent's feelings. Some kids withdraw, while others create more mischief. Others react with more angry outbursts, while others push their parents' buttons more to get some kind of reaction. Many negative cycles get started if this happens.

Have we convinced you of the importance of taking care of you? This is not self centered Me, Me, Me thinking. It is about taking care of yourself for the purpose of keeping yourself energized and balanced so you have more love and energy to give to your loved ones. It is easier to give to others when you are full rather than empty. Our kids need a model of keeping life in a healthy balance. The people they are most intently watching are mom and dad.

Ways To Take Care Of Ourselves

First, put taking care of yourself near the top of your list, not the bottom; because there will always be someone who needs a ride or a sandwich. Build in some regular, nurturing habits. Here are a few suggestions:

1. Quiet, Reflective Time

The best time for most people is first thing in the morning, although for some night-owls, it could be late at night when everyone else is in bed. Many people have found sunrise to be the most peaceful and quiet time of the day.

For the past four to five years I have taken 15-30 minutes each morning to meditate. I have a little quiet corner of our dining room by a window where I have a little meditation-type chair, some books with spiritual sayings, and a few statues. I have found that overall if I keep true to my daily quiet times, that I am much calmer and more patient.

T.J.

Some people use this time to read the Bible or listen to imagery tapes, motivational tapes, or read other spiritual books. It really will set the tone for your day.

2. Exercise

This can be as simple as walking four to five times a week to working out at the gym several times a week. It might require you to work out before your spouse leaves for work or maybe you could work out after work and arrive 45 minutes later, but it is well worth it.

I've been playing basketball with a group of guys at church every Tuesday night for eight years. I do not make them all, but I've learned to mark Tuesday nights off on my calendar six months ahead of schedule to avoid scheduling other things that would cause me to miss my best sweat of the week.

T.J.

I wish I could say I do something athletic, but the truth is, I am not an athletic person, and if I was, there have been times when we only had one car and I would have had trouble getting to a gym or a game. I tried to set up an exercise program in my home and we even bought some exercise equipment. Finally, I came to something that works very well for me. Every morning as soon as I wake up, I go in the office and do some simple exercises. I don't get dressed, I don't even put in my contacts, or turn on a lot of lights. (If I wake up, I might decide not to do it!) I just walk in there, half asleep and do a few stretches so I will not pull any muscles. After that I do a variety of things like leg lifts, thigh exercises, tummy crunches and more stretching, ending up with deep breathing and laying on my back thinking about all the good things I will be doing that day. This is my little time by myself, even though it is only for about 15 minutes. It does not turn me into a finely sculpted hardbody, but it does make me feel a little bit better about myself and gives me a good start to the day.

S.T.R.

3. Quiet Time In Nature

Nature is where people have always gone for solitude and reflection. Find some woods, a creek, a lake or a park nearby where you can go alone or with your family. Everything tends to slow down when you are out in nature.

4. Get The Most Out Of The Simple Pleasures In Life

Watch a sunset, fly a kite, star-gaze, bird watch, tinker in your garden, sit around a campfire, take a picnic. Do it regularly, not occasionally.

5. Let The Week Go

We know about one couple who every Friday night take a bubble bath together. They talk about their week, vent their frustrations, then watch as the water and their week goes down the drain. Great metaphor for letting go.

T.J.

6. Nurture Your Friendships

Phone calls, cards and random acts of kindness go a long way to maintaining your friendships. There are times when we need someone to talk to or lean on outside our

house and you will feel more comfortable doing that if you have been regularly keeping up with the friendship.

Spending time in nature with you can have a lasting imression on a child.

7. Nurture Your Marriage

This means more than collapsing together into bed at the end of a long, hectic day. The little things mean the most. Hugs, holding hands, surprise notes of gratitude or love, unexpected phone calls, back rubs and foot massages. These are all free and take but a few moments. They can mean the world to your tired partner.

For our 10 year wedding anniversary, I decided to surprise Anne with her dream vacation. I used our frequent flyer miles to book two tickets to Hawaii. I planned the entire trip, down to undoing her appointments and packing her bags and arranging for our babysitter. I even got her aunt to take her to breakfast the morning of our departure, then tell her they had to drive to the airport to pick up some lost luggage. Anne was speechless when her aunt drove up to the airport and there I was on the curb with her carry-on bag. I refused to tell her where we were going until we walked to the plane. She still says the best part of the entire week's vacation was how special she felt and cared for because I had taken care of all the details for her.

T.J.

I have been married to Rob for 15 years, and sadly, we have seen some of our good friends go through divorces along the way. They seem so much happier when they find new spouses and suddenly seem energized with a new outlook on life. Probably the reason Rob and I have had such a great relationship is that he treats me like a second wife. That's the best rookie advice I can give any couple- no matter how long you have been married, or how many times--treat your spouse like it's the second time around and it will always be exciting.

S.T.R.

8. Volunteer Work

This may sound crazy when you are flying by the seat of your pants, but we know of no better way to feel grounded and fulfilled than when we are giving of ourselves to others. If you can find a cause you have a passion for it will be all that much better. This kind of giving energizes us. Include your family so it is also a time together.

One summer I mentioned to my two sons about how fun it would be for them to find a place to volunteer for the summer. I ended up getting a six week job as a director of a day camp for three to five year olds. My sons were my volunteer counselors. It was so much fun to see them working with the kids. They learned a lot, gained new confidence in themselves, and we all had a blast working together.

S.T.R.

9. Do What Makes You Feel Better

Sometimes it just makes you feel better to get a new hairdo or a new outfit. You don't need to go crazy, but on the other hand, you should not martyr yourself. If you really want to cover that gray, go out and buy yourself a rinse and try it; it might lift your spirits. On the other hand, if you don't mind the gray, but you'd really like to try cutting it short, do it. A pretty color of lipstick can brighten your mood, or a nice golf shirt can make you feel like a million bucks. Surprise yourself every once in a while, while you are surprising your family.

A French Manicure You Can Afford

Some women martyr themselves to save money. You can do small things for yourself without spending much money. If you would like a French Manicure, but do not have the money to go to a fancy nail salon, go to the drug store and buy a kit and do it yourself. You can really save money if you just buy white, light pink, and clear.

Directions For A Do-It-Yourself French Manicure:

File and clean your nails. Apply a thin coat of light pink polish and let it dry. Take the white polish and do your tips. Look at someone who has it professionally done and you can figure out how to paint them. If you get some on your fingers, just wipe it off quickly before it dries. You should give your tips two coats at least. Be sure to really let it dry. The last thing to do is apply a clear, shiny coat of polish. You may want to use two coats of clear. There you have it— a French Manicure—just like the movie stars.

A Facial You Can Afford

Wish you could go to one of those spas and get a facial? Well, here's the next best thing. If you do this once a week you will feel rejuvenated. It will make you feel special if you have somewhere to go some evening.

Directions For A Do-It-Yourself Facial:

Wash your face and rinse with warm water. If you have long hair, you will want to pull it back. Spread honey all over your face. (yes, just regular honey from the cabinet) Leave it on for 15 minutes. (Just enough time to prop a pillow on your bed and look at a magazine!) Rinse it off with more warm water. First use your hands, then use a warm wash cloth. Now you can give yourself a sauna treatment. If you skip the sauna, rinse with cold water.

For a really special sauna: Boil some water, and set the pan on a placemat or hot pad. Take a large towel and cover your head with it. Lean down closer to the water and the steam will come up into your face. Try to keep out the other air and light by moving the towel. Take deep breaths and let the steam penetrate your face causing you to sweat. When you begin to get too hot, take off the towel and rinse your face with cold water. Apply a moisturizer. You will really feel relaxed.

Practice Your Golf Putting At Home
It would be great if you could get out to the driving range or golf course and practice your stroke, wouldn't it? Because of limited time or money you have been staying away. Why not set a tin can on its side and practice your putting in your living room? This could be something you would do by yourself, or you could do it with the kids. There are also golf videos you can rent and watch at home. You can get golf whiffle balls and practice driving them in the backyard or up the street at the park. If golf is something you really like to do, there are ways to be able to do it.

So Now Will You Take Care Of Yourself?
You get the idea from all of the suggestions we have given you. There are many more ways to take care of yourself and your marriage. They should be high in your priority list. Your state of mind and the tone of your marriage is the foundation from which everything else flows in your home. Everything runs smoother and calmer when we feel loved, full, rested, calm and peaceful.

If your home seems to be getting too hectic and there is constantly a stressful aura in it, take the time to calm it down. You deserve to live in a calm, peaceful, environment and so does your family. Talk about these things at family meetings or just with each other. Do whatever you need to do to not allow stress to take over your lives.

When we do things regularly and daily to take care of ourselves it is much easier to stay on top of things.

Remember that the best way to keep our kids grounded when the family is running all over is for *us* to stay grounded. We deserve it and so do our kids.

Chapter 21
Your Family—Sometimes
They're All You've Got

Your family is the most important natural resource you have and you should try every day to preserve it. As children grow up, they tend to spend more time away from their family as they go out into the world. If you have provided them with a good, stable family life, they will not usually stray far or for long. A job may take them to another town, but those with warm family memories will always look forward to the times they can spend with their families. During every episode in our lives, our family's support is important. It is important to support your family in good times and in bad times. By bringing children up from a young age with the notion of the importance of family, you are providing them with an extra security that many people in this transient and hectic world never get to experience.

Go To Their Shows

If it is at all possible, take off work for a few hours to go see the third grade play. That feeling your daughter will get when she sees you walk into the gym is something she will not forget when she grows up. Everybody wants to be supported. If you attend class plays, musical concerts, or ballgames you are showing your children that they are important, special and loved.

It is true that many tee-ball games can be about as exciting as watching grass grow. Watching your child out in the outfield kicking the grass, looking around, and basically doing everything except paying attention to the game can be frustrating; but when he comes off the field and sees you and you slap him five, you both feel a pride that is priceless and worth the hours of sitting on the bleachers. He also feels happy and secure. Even the kid that dropped the ball that provided the game winning run to the other team feels a little comfort in the fact that his parents are at the game, rather than having to walk home or get a ride home and ponder it all alone.

Sometimes as a parent we just have to be rushed and flustered and dash out after a meeting, and eat fast food in the car in order to get to something that is special to our kids. It may not seem like you are doing anything special when you rush from place to place so you can make it to your kid's game, but down the road, your child will remember the support he had or did not have. What you are doing for your children is what they will do for their children. You are setting an example for them.

Have a Catch, Dad

In the movie *Field of Dreams*, Ray Kinsella regretted that when his father asked him to "have a catch" he did not do it. His father asked him to go outside in the yard and play catch but he was too busy or did not want to do it. Harry Chapin, in his song "Cats in the Cradle" talks about a similar feeling but from the parent's perspective.

My son turned ten just the other day,
He said 'Thanks for the ball dad, come on let's play.
Can you teach me to throw?"
I said, 'Not today, I've got a lot to do."
He said, 'That's okay,"
And he smiled as he turned and walked away
And said, "I'm gonna be like him..."

Harry Chapin

The song is a father's lament at not having spent any quality time with his son. He bought him a baseball but did not take the time to play catch. Playing catch only takes five minutes if that is all the time you have. Right when you get home from work and before you have dinner, make the time to throw to your son who wants to play. The same goes for other interests of your children's. If your daughter likes to shoot baskets, shoot a few hoops with her. You do not have to spend a long time if you do not have it, but if you manage to squeeze it in, you

Whether it's playing catch or playing with dolls, it's important to spend time with your children doing things they like to do.

will be showing the child that he or she is important.

Playing cards is an excellent way of spending fun time with your child. There are so many different card games that there is one to fit everyone's needs. For very young children, just use 12 or 16 cards and play Concentration. (The old memory game where you try to turn two cards up to get a match, then it is the next person's turn to try to find a match).

As they get older, teach them War. This is where you divide the deck in half and take turns laying a card out, high card takes them both, then you lay another card, and so on. It's a quick game where younger kids can play at the same level as older siblings or parents.

You can progress on to Crazy Eights and then more difficult games like Rummy and Gin. Playing cards helps children with hand-eye coordination, it helps them with their numbers, helps them with patterns and sorting. There are so many things you are actually teaching your children when you are playing cards with them, but the best thing is that you are willing to take a few minutes out of your time to play with them.

If the evening has been a hectic one, either with activities or homework or maybe you have been busy with a project from work and have not been able to spend much time with your children, why not play a round of cards before bedtime. You can announce "at 7:30 we will play a round of Crazy Eights at the dining room table, so get your homework and your baths done before 7:30." This will give the children the heads up as to what is expected of them. Make sure you live up to the time you set even if you are in the middle of something. Decide on a designated time you will end the game (no matter who is winning) and end it at that time so they can go to bed. It is a nice, happy way to end an evening.

Always remember that the time you invest in your family is something that will come back to you with great interest. Be sure that in spending time with your children you remember to spend special quality time with your spouse if you are married. The entire time you are married, you should be cultivating your marriage as you would a prized African Violet. The more you put into it, the more beautiful it will become and grow.

This poem is worth reading and keeping. Though it says "my son," you can substitute various words in the poem for daughter, parent, friend, anyone you want to be sure to take the time to appreciate. Perhaps you would like to copy the poem and keep it where you will see it as a constant reminder. It is a beautifully written poem which comes straight from the heart.

To My Grown Up Son
by Alice E. Chase
My hands were busy through the day
I didn't have much time to play
The little games you asked me to,
I didn't have much time for you.
I'd wash your clothes; I'd sew and cook,
But when you'd bring your picture book
I'd say, " A little later, son."
I'd tuck you in all safe at night,
And hear your prayers, turn out the light,
Then tiptoe softly to the door,
I wish I'd stayed a minute more.
For life is short and years rush past,
A little boy grows up so fast.
No longer is he at your side,
His precious secrets to confide.

> The picture books are put away,
> There are no children's play,
> No goodnight kiss; no prayers to hear,
> That all belongs to yesteryear.
> My hands once busy, now lie still,
> The days are long and hard to fill,
> I wish I might go back and do,
> The little things you asked me to.

Remember that no one on their deathbed ever says they wish they would have spent more time at the office. You will never regret the times you spent playing with your children.

Sometimes it really "cramps your style" to play with your kids. A writer who has spent hours at the computer and the words are flowing easily has a hard time pulling away to meet her son at the front door and sit down to eat a snack with him and talk about how school went that day. It would be so much easier to call "hello" from the other room and keep working. Even if you get up from what you are doing for 15 minutes and then go back it will be precious time with your child. Chances are he will want to play outside with his friends anyway and you can go back to work.

Take Time Out For Your Children Every Day Of Your Life

The most important thing to remember when you are trying to keep your kids grounded when you are flying by the seat of your pants is to put your children first; to constantly and consciously be aware of their developmental and emotional

Teach your son to tie his tie, teach your daughter to tie her shoe. Taking time out of your schedule sends positive signals to your children.

needs; to understand that you are their primary role models and sources of love and acceptance and nurturing. It is a blessing and a responsibility to have a child. Keep doing your best and be willing to listen to your children for feedback about what their needs are at each stage and age. They deserve this kind of care and attention. If your family goes through time with a full goodwill account, you have ensured that your relationship with each other will continue along after they leave the nest.

About The Authors

Dr. Tim Jordan

Tim Jordan, M.D. spent two years of fellowship training in Developmental and Behavioral Pediatrics, the second year at the Child Development Unit at Harvard Medical School learning from Dr. T. Berry Brazelton, after earning his M.D. from the University of Missouri-Columbia School of Medicine and completing a three year pediatric residency.

Tim has counseled children, teens, couples, and families for 15 years. He and his wife, Anne, founded Children and Families, Inc. out of which they have taught parenting classes, couples communication classes, weekend personal growth retreats for adults, teens and couples and self-esteem building summer camps for children and teenagers.

Dr. Jordan is a national speaker who has spoken to parents, teachers, professionals and corporations in over 30 states since 1985. He is the author of the book <u>What I Learned At Summer Camp About Understanding And Loving Our Children</u>, as well as numerous articles for newspapers and magazines. Tim and his wife have been married for 18 years and are the proud parents of three children: Kelly, 16; T.J., 14; and John, 10.

Sally Tippett Rains

Sally Tippett Rains is an author and the mother of two boys. She has been a Cub Scout Leader for the last six years, as well as a classroom volunteer, youth league parent, church youth group leader, Bible School co-director, charity fund-raiser volunteer, and day camp director. She has authored five books: <u>The Insider's Guide To The Pope's Visit To St. Louis</u>, with David Klocek; <u>Youth Baseball, A Coaches and Parents Guide</u>, with Wendell Kim; <u>Drills and Skills for Youth Basketball</u>, with Rich Grawer; <u>Softball Pitching Fundamentals And Techniques</u>, with Carie Dever-Boaz; and <u>Playing On His Team</u>, which she co-wrote with her husband Rob Rains. The Rains family and their sons, B.J. and Mike live in St. Louis, Mo.

If you would like more information about Dr. Tim Jordan's company Children & Families, Inc. you can contact him at Children & Families, Inc., 444 Chesterfield Center, Suite 205, Chesterfield, MO 63017. For information about his camps and talks, call (636) 530-1883.

For information on other books by Sally Tippett Rains, visit www.rainsmedia.com.

BOOKS AND TAPES AVAILABLE FROM
PALMERSTON & REED

Mass Market Series

Insider's Guide to the Pope's Visit to St. Louis, Missouri, USA
by David Klocek & Sally Rains
A memorable book about Pope John Paul II and his 1999 visit to St. Louis. Illustrated. Soft-cover.
Item #1-300-01 $7.95

Keeping Your Kids Grounded When You're Flying By The Seat of Your Pants
by Tim Jordan, M.D. & Sally Tippett Rains
Practical ideas for meeting the universal challenges of parenting. Illustrated. Soft-cover.
Item #1-300-02 $14.95

Pushcarts & Stalls: The Soulard Market History Cookbook
by Suzanne Corbett
A culinary treasure of historical recipes from Soulard Market vendors and farm families and includes many of the author's heirloom family recipes. Illustrated. Soft-cover, wirebound.
Item #1-300-04 $16.95

Martial Arts Series

Advanced Karate-Do: Concepts, Techniques, and Training Methods
by Elmar T. Schmeisser, Ph.D.
An invaluable technical resource book that clearly and concisely analyzes the advanced concepts of Shotokan-style karate. Illustrated. Soft-cover.
Item #1-200-01 $16.50

Bunkai: Secrets of the Karate Kata
by Elmar T. Schmeisser, Ph.D.
Hidden secrets of karate techniques in easy-to-understand
sequences. Illustrated. Soft-cover.
Item #1-200-02 $17.95

Conversations with the Master: Masatoshi Makayama
by Randall G. Hassell
Exclusive, in-depth interview with the late headmaster of the
Japan Karate Association as he describes his early training and
talks extensively about modern karate. Illustrated. Soft-cover.
Item #1-200-03 $12.95

Karate Ideals
by Randall G. Hassell
Examines the philosophical, historical, and societal influences
on the martial arts of the samurai. Illustrated. Soft-cover.
Item #1-200-04 $12.95

The Karate Spirit
by Randall G. Hassell
A selected collection of essays that provides invaluable information about the art of traditional karate. Soft-cover.
Item #1-200-05 $12.95

Karate Training Guide Volume 1: Foundations of Training
by Randall G. Hassell
An illustrated guide to the basic techniques and philosophy of
karate training to help you understand the fundamentals of
Shotokan-style karate. Illustrated. Soft-cover.
Item #1-200-06 $12.95

Karate Training Guide Volume 2: Kata Heian, Tekki, Bassai Dai
by Randall G. Hassell
Complete, simple, move-by-move instructions plus detailed analysis of selected moves to help you practice and study the first nine formal exercises of Shotokan-style karate. Illustrated. Soft-cover.
Item #1-200-07 $12.95

Meeting Myself: Beyond Spirit of the Empty Hand
by Stan Schmidt
The autobiography of the world's highest-ranking, non-Japanese Japan Karate Association master. Illustrated. Soft-cover.
Item #1-200-08 $17.95

Modern Karate: Scientific Approach to Conditioning and Training
by Milorad Stricevic, Dusan Dacic, Toyotaro Miyazaki, George Anderson
Learn how to achieve peak conditioning and unbeatable competition skills. Illustrated. Hard-cover.
Item #1-200-09 $40.00

New Students in Karate: The First Three Months
by Merlin T. Taylor, Jr.
Answers the most commonly asked questions about traditional karate training. Soft-cover.
Item#1-200-10 $9.95

Recognition: A Novel
by Stan Schmidt
"Recognition" is a story for all aspiring athletes and especially young people traveling a road of life full of obstacles and disappointments. Soft-cover.
Item #1-200-11 $8.95

Samurai Journey
by Randall G. Hassell & Osamu Ozawa
Follow the remarkable story of Osamu Ozawa, the most senior
Shotokan instructor in the Western world, including his samurai
upbringing, crashing as a kamikaze pilot, his run as a successful
TV director, decline into poverty, and his final triumph as a
karate master. Illustrated. Soft-cover.
Item #1-200-12 $17.95

Shotokan Karate: Its History and Evolution
     (Revised & Illustrated)
by Randall G. Hassell
A recently updated edition of the first comprehensive written
history of Shokotan karate – in any language. Illustrated. Soft-
cover.
Item #1-200-13 $15.95

Spirit of the Empty Hand
by Stan Schmidt
The fascinating true story of the author's journey to 3rd degree
black belt in Japan. Illustrated. Soft-cover.
Item #1-200-14 $15.95

Zen, Pen and Sword: The Karate Experience
by Randall G. Hassell
The spiritual, intellectual, and physical dimensions of karate,
bringing to life the essence of traditonal martial arts. Soft-cover.
Item #1-200-15 $15.95

Martial Arts Video Tapes

Soul of Karate – Original Director's Cut
Featuring Stan Schmidt
Contains some of the most exciting karate footage ever shot of
traditional karate training conducted in the rugged South
African way. "This tape shows what the true karate spirit is
about. Every instructor must see it," says Masatoshi Nakayama,
late Headmaster of the Japan Karate Association.
Item#1-400-01 $34.95

The Winning Blow
Featuring the World's Most Famous Karata-ka in Action
This fast-paced, half-hour program includes footage of more
than two dozen karate masters from the All-Japan and World
Championships. Narrated by Stan Schmidt. 30 minutes.
Item#1-400-02 $19.95

Stan Schmidt Instructs Shotokan Karate
Volume 1 – Beginner Level
Provides easy-to-follow demonstrations and applications of
basic techniques, basic five-step sparring, katas 1 and 2, applications of kata moves, and more of Shotokan-style karate by the
world's highest ranking Western instructor.
Item#1-400-03 $39.95

Stan Schmidt Instructs Shotokan Karate
Volume 2 – Intermediate Level
Includes combination techniques, 1-step sparring, throws, holds,
and more. Featuring Japan Karate Association World Champion
Pavlo Protopappa and a special appearance by professional
golfer Bobby Verwey, Jr.
Item #1-400-04 $39.95

Stan Schmidt Instructs Shotokan Karate
Volume 3 – Advanced Level
Designed for students and instructors. Includes advanced basic
techniques, advanced 1-step and semi-free sparring, self-
defense, breaking, and more. Featuring more than 12 South
African National, International, and World Champions.
Item #1-400-05 $39.95

TO ORDER
Call toll free 1-877-99-BOOKS
Or visit our website at www.palmerston.com